NORMAN MAILER
The Countdown
(The First Twenty Years)

Donald L. Kaufmann

WITH A PREFACE BY

Harry T. Moore

SOUTHERN ILLINOIS UNIVERSITY PRESS
Carbondale and Edwardsville

FEFFER & SIMONS, INC.
London and Amsterdam

For Cheryl

Crosscurrents/MODERN CRITIQUES

Harry T. Moore, *General Editor*

Preface

Norman Mailer is so often thought of as a kind of enfant terrible that it is good, just now, to have a serious consideration of his writing. And Donald L. Kaufmann, in Norman Mailer: The Countdown, provides the kind of study that we need.

He takes the first twenty years of Mailer's career, up to 1966. This means that he omits a discussion of one novel, Why are We in Vietnam? (the least important of Mailer's imaginative works), as well as of the two recent books of current history, The Armies of the Night (winner of a 1969 National Book Award) and Miami and the Siege of Chicago. These last two are admittedly important, if only as superior journalism, but they contain nothing which would essentially affect Kaufmann's judgments on Mailer's most important fiction.

He gives serious consideration to The Naked and the Dead, hailed in 1948 as the finest American novel of World War II, as well as to Barbary Shore and The Deer Park, neither of them greeted at first with enthusiasm, though they are novels which have survived across the years.

Donald Kaufmann also deals with various other aspects of Norman Mailer, such as his socio-political beliefs and his detachment from America's "Jewish Renaissance."

But the achievement of Mailer's which attracts most of Kaufmann's attention is the novel An Amer-

ican Dream, *originally serialized in* Esquire. *Kaufmann
shows that this book has roots in Theodore Dreiser's*
An American Tragedy, *and he examines it not only
in a chapter devoted to the novel itself, but also in
the section entitled "The Hero on the Existential
Make." (Although in my review of* An American
Dream, *at the time the book came out, I mentioned
certain resemblances to Dostoevsky's* Crime and
Punishment, *no one seems to have taken up the idea
—but certainly there is a parallel between Rojack's
relations with the investigating detective and those
of Roskolnikov with the examining magistrate in the
earlier novel.)*

Donald Kaufmann subtitles his book The Countdown, *for reasons which he gives in his Introduction.
The reader will of course note that, in countdown
style, the ten chapters are numbered in reverse order.*

*I want to repeat that we are in Donald L. Kauf-
mann's debt for this serious and excellent study of
Norman Mailer's work. His importance as a novelist—
and let us hope he will give us more fiction in the
future—is capably demonstrated here, and this book
is a valuable contribution to the understanding of
today's literature.*

HARRY T. MOORE

Southern Illinois University
March 2, 1969

Acknowledgments

Quotations from *The Deer Park, The Presidential Papers,* and *An American Dream* reprinted by permission of the Author and his Agents, Scott Meredith Literary Agency, Inc., 580 Fifth Avenue, New York, N. Y.

Extracts by Norman Mailer from *Cannibals and Christians.* Copyright © 1966 by Norman Mailer. Reprinted by permission of the author and his agents, Scott Meredith Literary Agency, Inc., 580 Fifth Avenue, New York, N. Y.

Quotations reprinted by permission of G. P. Putnam's Sons from *Advertisements For Myself* by Norman Mailer. Copyright © 1959 by Norman Mailer; also by permission of André Deutsch Limited, 105 Great Russell Street, London.

Quotations reprinted from *An American Dream* by Norman Mailer. Copyright © 1964, 1965 by Norman Mailer and used by permission of the publisher, The Dial Press, Inc.

Quotations reprinted by permission of G. P. Putnam's Sons from *The Deer Park* by Norman Mailer. Copyright 1955 by Norman Mailer.

Quotations reprinted by permission of G. P. Putnam's Sons from *The Presidential Papers* by Norman Mailer. Copyright © 1960, 1961, 1962, 1963 by Norman Mailer.

Quotations from "An Interview with Norman Mailer" reprinted from *Mademoiselle*; Copyright © 1961 by the Condé Nast Publications Inc.

Quotations reprinted from *The Naked and The Dead* and *Barbary Shore* by permission of Norman Mailer.

"Mailer in Provincetown," Author-Interview Tape Library, ed: Edmund Skellings

"Mailer in Alaska," Author-Interview Tape Library, ed: Edmund Skellings

My personal acknowledgment to Dr. Edmund Skellings, poet-professor at Florida Atlantic University, who first suggested this study, who first introduced me to Mailer, who stayed with this book from Iowa to Alaska to Florida, and who is one of the few who can wrestle with Mailer in elevators without ever coming down.

D. L. K.

Contents

Key for Abbreviations

All page references are to the following books, which are thus abbreviated:

AD	*An American Dream*
ADV.	*Advertisements for Myself*
BS	*Barbary Shore*
CC	*Cannibals and Christians*
DP	*The Deer Park*
ND	*The Naked and the Dead*
PP	*The Presidential Papers*
	Also
SI	Skellings Interview

These abbreviations are used only when cited source changes. Otherwise only the page reference is given.

Introduction: *ADVERTISEMENT FOR INTENT*

On the current American literary scene, Norman Mailer sticks out, alone, with his knack for controversy, even far out of the literary establishment. Today there is a fringe of the public that has never read a single Mailer word and yet know him as that writer hellbent on exhibitionism. Such a literary figure, who receives equal billing in critical periodicals and daily tabloids, creates such confusion that it becomes almost impossible to separate the man, Norman Mailer, from his work. Various public and private images of Mailer converge into a central blur.

From the literary world, opinions spring up about Mailer like funnel clouds, streaked with love and hate. Some spokesmen claim that Mailer began as a most promising talent, but has since gone to seed as a minor journalist and novelist, whose footnote in American literary history will read—a flashy first novelist of 1948. Another critical group (one hundred per cent hawk) cries "overrated," and says that Mailer has always been a do-nothing, no-talented writer who acts like the noisy adolescent of American letters. But for almost every detractor, there is a literary opinion somewhere between so-so praise and open acclaim. Mailer's partisans divide themselves into two groups. The first has always regarded him either as the most important or as one of the most significant writers to appear after World War II. Yet this group—thinking a great talent has fallen off in pulp fiction or slick magazines—concedes that Mailer's future lies behind him. The second group, Mailer's authentic disciples, focus instead on his aesthetic potential, insisting that no matter how great were Mailer's achievements in the past, they were but previews of even greater happenings in his future. In this view, Mailer is on the brink of becoming the chief literary representative of his age.

All this ado about how bad (or evil?) or how good is Norman Mailer is a fascinating side show, in which serious criticism turns into an art of ambivalence. I call it a side show because it never bears down on the main issue—is Mailer's work really worth all this controversy? The word on Mailer, thus far, is criticism without a cause, keeping time to Mailer's non-literary adventures—a stabbing, divorces, drugs, arrests, fist fights, and other special effects, which make his life as intriguing as his art. In the absence of thorough criticism of his work, ambivalence runs the show. It is sometimes difficult to sift praise from scorn in the same paragraph, even the same sentence written by the same critic. Usually, a review of a Mailer book passes into a critique on Mailer the man. A writer who can pass for a hoodlum can give a scholar the jitters. Mailer-itis also carries over to anyone well-read in Mailer. In some universities and publishing houses there is the so-called "Mailer man" in a limbo between awe and ridicule. If provoked, he will take on the airs of a tough guy, as he either defends or attacks Hemingway's heir apparent. Who else but Mailer has this knack for so much attraction or repulsion. I can think of no other current writer criticized by so many minds made up too soon. At present, Mailer's work seems vulnerable to everything but a thorough analysis.

That is my intention. To do this, my approach to Mailer must avoid what may come too naturally. I will not do a survey of Mailer criticism—something like "Mailer and his Critics"—which would probably end up telling more about the critics than Mailer. Nor will I attempt (however tempting) to follow the lead of some critics and reviewers who insert Mailer into some niche in American literary history. I must go along with first-things-first—an extended critical analysis of his work, and then, a study of his place in literary history.

The most natural way not to approach Mailer—a critical biography—remains till last. In terms of sale potential, I would imagine such a book would go light on stuffy criticism and heavy on lurid biography (the ins and outs of a wife-stabbing, alone worth its weight in print). The biographical approach to Mailer is the easiest way for a critic to get lost in a subjective maze of truth for sale in tabloids. Even Mailer's "muted autobiography" in *Advertisements* is too "muted." Filled with an incredible amount of what it was to be a writer at that time, *Advertisements* may become a standard source for studying the plight of the American writer during the Fifties, and yet—in terms of any later definitive biography—Mailer's personality may turn out to be the most startling piece of fiction in the book. Until Mailer finds more psychic distance between his life and his art, what passes for his biography will only mess up the core of my book. For this reason, I will do away with as much of the biographical approach as is possible. Only toward the end, will biography come on the scene—my concession to the present fact that only a miracle can separate Mailer as writer from Mailer as man.

What also makes Mailer a special case is his sheer unpredictability. As a kind of chameleon of American letters, he sticks to the new, and keeps at bay his horror of a second time around with either subject or method—change apparently for the sake of change. I will avoid the treadmill of constant revision by ignoring any Mailer work-in-progress during 1967. I will limit my coverage to the period 1947–1966, the first twenty years of Mailer's career as writer and as cultural spokesman. Only at the end, will I (by choice) turn seer in a brief conclusion with its give-away title—"Early Last Words."

The first word on my projected book came from John Clellon Holmes (then teaching at the University of Iowa) who claimed that my research on Mailer would be similar to Marlow's voyage of discovery in Conrad's *Heart of Darkness*. I listened to Holmes tell how Mailer's vision took to the underside of American experience in the aftermath of Hiroshima and Dachau. Norman Mailer may not be a carbon copy of Mister Kurtz, but Mailer's vision—its stuff of sex, violence, psychopathy, incest, and other taboos—is fixed on the edge of a cultural abyss at the "heart" of American darkness. There was also an analogy in the temptation (that almost takes over Marlow, Conrad's narrator) to identify with the voice at the abyss —in my case, to identify with the mass of attraction and repulsion that surrounds Mailer's voice. Holmes's final word was that I could turn into a kind of Marlow, sidetracked to a defense or an attack, whose own voice would be lost in either Mailer or his critics.

To be as thorough and as objective as possible, my book on Mailer—in a sense—must begin at the end. I call it my "countdown" on Mailer's work—from literature as such, to literature as public statement, and finally, to literature as private vision. By doing first-things-first, I can finally zero in on where literature, milieu, and personality converge, at the heart of the controversy that sticks to Mailer. From my first chapter (numbered last) to my conclusion, "I" will drop out. I will take no part in any "cult of personality," including my own. My disappearing "I" should be all the more obvious when set alongside Mailer's ubiquitous "I"—a sign (if I may show the end at the beginning) that Mailer has lost his voice at the abyss, much like Kurtz, whose once loud and clear voice has been reduced to a whisper of "the horror."

NORMAN MAILER: The Countdown

The Vision and the Beast
in Peace and War

Despite Mailer's reputation as a novelist with two "first" novels, his earliest fiction reveals a basic vision which lends unity to what is otherwise Mailer's two fresh starts—a fictive world based on alienation, anxiety, and atavism. This condition of modern man is a constant in the two books.

War is the collective image for Mailer's earliest portrayal of his vision. While *The Naked and the Dead* impressed the literary public as the first important World War II novel, Mailer claims: "I intended it to be a parable about the movement of man through history. I tried to explore the outrageous propositions of cause and effect, of effort and recompense, in a sick society" (*New Yorker*, October 23, 1948). This enlarges the novel's scope to include much more than a representation of war.

The novel uses the strategy of the microcosm. Here the little world, the military campaign on the tiny island of Anopopei, represents the entire Pacific war theatre, or any war at any time. Mailer's strategy also concerns the military unit. The macrocosmic army— the universal world of regimented men—is depicted in the image of an intelligence and reconnaissance (I and R) unit. Episodes centering at headquarters, with its white-collar atmosphere, are spaced between scenes that show the infantry beset with drudgery and grime. Mailer keeps stressing how disconnected these little worlds are. Not only has communication broken down vertically, between officers and enlisted men, it has failed horizontally. General Cummings and Major Dalleson are as estranged as the corporals and privates. Even when personalities are somewhat similar —the psychopathic and efficient General Cummings and Sergeant Croft, or the sensitive and inept Lieutenant Hearn and Private Valsen—the vertical bar due to rank prevents any mutual understanding. As a little map mirroring vaster ones, Anopopei is an isolated island, subject only to the laws of war.

War keeps a man from knowing his fellows and it also confuses him in respect to time. In a sense, war provides him with a new calendar. The wartime hours, days, weeks and months cause soldiers to reappraise their past. Peacetime concerns such as ambitions, hopes, jobs and loves would have been evaluated and affirmed in a society not totally a part of an atmosphere which threatens immediate extinction. Since man's initial need for time-division is a way of acknowledging his mortality, a belief in the greater probability of his own death can alter his sense of the present. During a war, every moment verges on the last. Living in the present becomes oppressive while living for the future becomes absurd. As a result the past almost imperceptibly acquires the temporal content of the present—a fact of war that confronts Mailer's soldiers. Already ensnared in a spatial prison, they begin to tell time by the calendar on its walls. Confused by their wartime visions, officers and common soldiers alike increasingly fail to distinguish between peacetime and wartime. Yesterday and yesterday's futures give way to what Mailer would term the "enormous present." Near the novel's conclusion, Mailer inserts a "Mute Chorus" entitled "On what we do when we get out" which drones out GI fantasies, a chorus which Mailer "mutes" with the following preface: "Sometimes spoken, usually covert, varying with circumstance." The concept of time "varying with circumstance" also shapes the numerous "Time Machines." Throughout these snap surveys of the various

characters' pasts, there is a tendency to portray peacetime as an inverted form of war. As omniscient author, Mailer imprints each past with the soldier's present consciousness. Cities and hometowns are now
characterized by settings so filthy that friend and
neighbors act like animals in a jungle. Past journeys
are reinterpreted as dreaded uprootings. Ambitions,
once considered a sure way to success, are now recast
into treacherous symptoms of eternal futility. Apart
from the "Time Machines," memories are also re-
shaped. Many soldiers can no longer recall their loves,
and their imaginations keep accusing wives or lovers
of sexual infidelity. Letters are addressed "Dear John."
The most dramatic examples of such letters are those
Gallagher receives, after much postal delay, from his
wife, who has since died in childbirth. The Mailer
soldiers distort time, and time distorts itself—a displacement in time to match the dislocation in space.

The theme of a world at war sets up the title.
Mailer has stated (*Current Biography,* 1948) that the
term "Naked" refers both to the "war-mongering fa-
natics" and to the men "whose minds are so tainted."
But Mailer's image of uniformed men being stripped
also accents the more universal implication.

> In the author's eyes, *The Naked and the Dead* is not a
> realistic documentary; it is, rather, a "symbolic" book,
> of which the basic theme is the conflict between the
> beast and the seer in man. The number of events
> experienced by the one platoon couldn't possibly have
> happened to any one army platoon in the war, but
> represent a composite view of the Pacific war. The
> mountain the platoon attempts to climb represents
> death and man's creative urge, fate, man's desire to
> conquer the elements—all kinds of things that you
> never dream of separating and stating so baldly.

What Mailer more explicitly means by "the conflict
between the beast and the seer" is war's tendency to
reduce man to an animal existence and his repeated
attempts to reassert his humanity. Metaphorically the

clothes to be removed are civilization's. A man pre-
pared for war is at the outset made uncivilized (re-
leased from certain restraints), before being furnished
a weapon, and before being urged to commit violence
and murder sanctioned by society, state, and God.
Bestiality will result if the conditioning to wartime
behavior lasts long enough.

There are many allusions to man reverting to beast.
Dog eat dog, and a dogtag is hung around a man's
neck. Mailer's own fictional analogy (18) to Pavlov's
experiments with dogs points out another fact of war
—instead of a man fearing to become an animal, he is
more fearful of becoming a man and not surviving.
Embodied as beasts entering a world governed by
instinct, the soldiers can only dimly recall their displaced manhood. Above the enlisted man, higher in
the hierarchy of bestiality, the officers' style of atavism
is more refined. On reviewing his "relationship" with
General Cummings, Lieutenant Hearn can analyze
what those ranked lower can only feel: "He had been
the pet, the dog, to the master, coddled and curried,
thrown sweetmeats until he had had the presumption
to bite the master once. And since then he had been
tormented with the particular absorbed sadism that
most men could generate only toward an animal"
(313).

Despite the widespread brutishness, an occasional
humane value (always brief and futile) will emerge,
like Gallagher's mild Catholicism or Martinez's childlike patriotism. But usually the warrior's response to
the supernatural or the idealistic is either a terrified
awareness of some malignant force, such as that
"something . . . watching over their shoulder and
laughing" (39), or a simple dismissal, such as Polack's
epithet for God—"he sure is a sonofabitch" (607).
Within such godless stone walls, the symbolic network operating must elect a Cummings to the rank of
"seer," the prophet of eternal regimentation. Only the
General has enough intellect and experience to see the

bestiality on Anopopei in its historical prospective. By permitting a Cummings to come (to echo his name), a corrupt America has taken on the role of metaphorical tailor, stripping its people of civilian authority while reclothing its army with brute power. Lacking those tools of technology usually provided by civilization to subdue their natural environment, the soldiers must face nature on its own terms. The weather and the jungle are even more imposing than the enemy. Typhoons rage. Trails are knotted, intertwined. The rugged weather and terrain sap men's energy more insidiously than enemy bullets. Minus proper toilet facilities and other forms of sanitation, the infantrymen find the stench overpowering. Nature's and man's odors continue to intermingle until they merge. When the beachhead is established, Minetta quips, "Smell your own stink or get carried away by the bugs" (58). Only at the heights where there exists more soap, more vestiges of civilization, and more stars and bars, does the jungle serve any useful function. "Cummings had a sensation of being suspended in air . . . the jungle seemed to strip him of everything but the quick absorbed functioning of his mind" (105). In this instance, the human mind is at least busy "somewhere in space"—an example of what Mailer means by a theme focused on "death and man's creative urge, fate, man's desire to conquer the elements."

In *The Naked and the Dead* predetermined causal forces take over Anopopei. There is the ironic conclusion wherein the campaign for the island is won through the blind, lucky decisions of the fumbling, prosaic Major Dalleson, while Cummings, the master at strategy, is absent. War's chaos linked to inscrutable Nature shows up when Wilson's dead body is washed down a river, eluding the survival and burial which Ridges and Goldstein had hoped to accomplish after their ordeal as litter bearers. On Mount Anaka, the hornets' nest which ominously ruins Croft's quest to reach the summit also highlights Mailer's approach to "man's creative urge" and "man's desire to conquer the elements." Jungle warfare develops a creativity expressed in a coarser and cruder manner. Physical skills are superior to mental skills, with few exceptions. Brutish man discovers that his "creative urge" either compels him to be the annointed leader of the animal pack, as is the case with Cummings, or to conquer nature, the proving ground of the war itself. Already a sanctioned killer during peacetime, and presently satiated with violence and battle, Sergeant Croft yearns to become, in Polack's phrase (606), "an idealist." Looming above the ordinary challenges afforded men at war stands the almost insurmountable Mount Anaka. It stirs terror in nearly everyone, including the inept rebel, Lieutenant Hearn: "the mountain troubled him, roused his awe and then his fear. It was too immense, too powerful" (497). And when Hearn "peered into Croft," Mailer labels it, "look(ing) down into an abyss." Within the symbolic context, the "abyss," characterized by man's reversion to the beast, must possess a counterpart at the peak—man's highest possible attainment as an animal. And when climbing, Croft can sense his own instinctual destiny—"The sheer mass of the mountain inflamed him" (635). At the opposite extreme are the feelings of the men commanded to follow Croft on his quest: "They had discovered that they could not hate him and do anything about it, so they hated the mountain, hated it with more fervor than they could ever have hated a human being" (698). Unlike Croft, the ordinary soldier whose ambition is centered on staying alive, associates a god who must be a "sonofabitch" with one of his incarnations, the mountain. Their creative urge remains purely physiological. Croft instead views Anaka as "the inviolate elephant" (709), that ageless and uncharted territory, the map to all the animals' graveyards, revealing the prophetic answer to why mankind must interpret his history with periodic organized murder. A hornet-nest ends this probing into the abyss. Does this fateful conclusion satisfy Croft? "Deep down himself, Croft was relieved . . . was rested by the unadmitted knowledge that he had found a limit to his hunger" (701). Somewhere in his subconscious, Croft acknowledges his own inherent limitations. To become the seer in such a world is to acquire isolation, a select condition where knowledge coexists with instinct. Only Cummings has the mind to dare such a superhuman ascent. Relieved, Croft finally realizes it is better to remain below, to be the most competent beast in the abyss.

As part of the strategy of the wartime microcosm, the narrative pattern in *The Naked and the Dead* becomes an extended commentary on man's isolation from normal space and time and even from his own species. The action is divided into four parts: 1] the invasion of Anopopei; 2] the deadlocked campaign for the island; 3] the denouement, consisting of the sudden disintegration of the Japanese defense coupled with the exploits behind the enemy's lines of the "I and R" unit under the command of Hearn then Croft; and 4] the mopping-up operations and the return of the men and the island to ironic normality. Besides attempting to depict all the possible situations that men may encounter in battle, Mailer uses the extensive narrative to dramatize his various themes in multiple ways.

Also supplementing Mailer's themes is the large gallery of characters with "tainted minds." On Anopopei virtually every personality type from almost every geographical area in America is represented. A partial list includes: Wilson, Southern Cracker; Croft, psychopathic Texan; Gallagher, right-wing Irishman from Boston; Brown, All-American from Tulsa; Ridges, religious farmer from Mississippi; Martinez, Mexican from San Antonio; Polack, petty racketeer from Chicago; Goldstein, Jew from Brooklyn; and Valsen, drifter from Montana. At the higher echelons, the numbers diminish and geographical diffusion is less. Most of the officers, such as Lieutenant Colonels Webber and Conn (the one a gluttonous Dutchman, the other a bigot against Negroes and Jews), are not fully developed as characters. They function as a collective foil to the enlisted men—though victimized at the top, they still turn victimizers at the bottom. The exceptions are Cummings, the fascist philosopher, and Hearn, the misanthropic liberal. Products of small-town midwestern capitalism, both the General and the Lieutenant possess intellectual depth and are the two most complex characters in the novel. Whether ranked high or low, all the characters share the same imprisonment, the same predicament—disentangling the war with nature and the enemy from the war among and within themselves. For the officers, the crucial problem consists of retaining as much rationality as possible in a world adapted to the irrational. For the enlisted man, the dilemma lies in preserving as much personal identity as is possible in a world dedicated to mass obedience to the military. Unless remedies are pursued, unless the vestiges of civilization are strengthened, men will lapse into regimented pawns at the mercy of martial law.

Mailer's narrative accents the negative, demonstrating how the characters are drifting from "seer" to "beast," as the men gradually yield to the rule of instinct, heeding those promptings from the darker corridor of their souls, until the values of civilization pass away. In such an atavistic world only Cummings has any higher aspiration. His "psychological soundness," referring to his military genius, results from his "pathological adjustment" to a jungle world. Otherwise, throughout the ranks, mutual suspicion intensifying to hatred usually overcomes both officers and men. In contrast with this trend are minor examples of affection, integrity, trust, and other values more in style during peacetime. Included among these are Toglio's heartfelt and childlike patriotism; Martinez' in-

tense pride in his abilities as scout and soldier; Goldstein's genuine concern for his wife and their future;
and even the veteran Red Valsen's sentimentality toward Hennessey, the rookie preparing himself for battle. Usually such tendencies remain weak inside the
individual, and are never able to affect the group. At
other times, what begins as human hope changes into
animal despair. Toglio's buddies ridicule his patriotism. Hennessey's early death causes Valsen to become
"the loner." Croft makes an attempt at liking a man
on the squad—"the intimate look of old friends" between himself and Martinez—but he keeps waning to
indifference. In fact, total indifference toward the
others pays off with more success than failure. If ambition is to prevail, then conduct must follow the rules
of total egoism. Its embodiment is Stanley, the nine-
teen-year-old go-getter, who first mimics and cajoles
his superiors in order to attain their heights, only to
turn callous or ruthless toward any former superior
who cannot match his ruthlessness. Less adept and
motivated than Stanley, most of the others are assimilated into a group linked by a common discontent and
resentment. Their passing into the way of the "beast"
is made clear by the episode concerning the hunt,
undertaken by some drunken soldiers, for souvenirs
belonging to enemy corpses, dead long enough to
swell purple and green. In this instance, the dramatic
climax takes place when Martinez feels a "mixture of
guilt and glee" (214) as he smashes a corpse's mouth
and absconds with its gold teeth. In desecrating the
dead of his own species, man is shedding his own
identification as a human being. Mailer shows how
the "conflict between the beast and the seer" verges
on a fatal resolution—those times when the beast in
man seems powerful enough to become its own
"seer." At such times, brutish law reigns and the weak
cannot survive.

Probably the most intelligent and sensitive member
of the enlisted group is Roth. An office clerk misem-

ployed in the I and R unit, he continues to be treated as a misfit, ostracized until Croft's fanatic urge to conquer Mt. Anaka claims him as its sacrificial victim.

One criticism directed at Mailer's novel concerns its pessimism. But Mailer argues that "The book finds man corrupted, confused to the point of helplessness, but it also finds that there are limits beyond which he cannot be pushed, and it finds that even in his corruption and sickness there are yearnings for a better world" (*New Yorker*, October 23, 1948).

Throughout *The Naked and the Dead* the collective attitudes of the soldiers—their stock responses of cynicism, misogyny, bigotry and obscenity—almost conceal those more soulful and redeeming qualities innate to men everywhere. Mailer's soldiers display (though rarely and never as a group) inner resources of strength and determination not to yield to the nonhuman values. The episode depicting the valiant, though unsuccessful, endeavor at saving Wilson's life furnishes the most detailed and dramatic example of man's resistance to bestiality. On a reconnaissance mission behind enemy lines, Wilson is fatally wounded. Rather than abandon the amiable Southerner, Hearn and the squad reluctantly decide to carry the dying soldier on a litter over the tortuous trail from the mountain pass to the shoreline. Brown, Stanley, Ridges, and Goldstein are selected as the permanent litter-bearers. Their bodies ache and their minds turn delirious. But soon their acquired hatred toward the thankless task imposed by the army is replaced by "guilt and empathy, and the torments of his wound seemed to pass through the handles of the stretcher up into their arms" (624). This assimilation into a profound sympathy for a comrade's suffering renews those bonds which interlock men in an altruistic union. At first the loss of egoism within the stretcher-bearers is too sudden, since war has conditioned them to survive through selfishness. "Each of them was fighting his private battle" (625). And soon, two lack the necessary energy to continue seeking a higher existence than a beast in a jungle. Due to complete physical exhaustion, Brown and Stanley, the All-American Boy and the scheming go-getter, depart from their assignment, relinquishing their ordeal to Goldstein, a Brooklyn Jew, and Ridges, a Mississippi farmer who believes in God. For these two, existence heightens into a new awareness, "they were reduced to the lowest common denominator of their existence. Carrying him was the only reality they knew" (644). Empathy with prolonged dying promotes a distinct change within both soldiers. Even after Wilson dies, his body disappearing beneath the rapids, intensifying the absurdity and futility surrounding their ordeal, Goldstein and Ridges experience separate bitterness before attaining a mutual recognition. Finally on the beach they sprawl, unconsciously concerned for one another. Two soldiers, alone but paradoxically together, have shared a journey into an uncharted region, not on Croft's prophetic mountain, but on that psychic terrain that distinguishes man from beast. Brown and Stanley allow the army to define them, while Goldstein and Ridges define themselves.

Mailer also provides his readers with a hopeful footnote. The novel's ironic conclusion can be read as either pessimistic or optimistic. Just how much comfort a reader can muster from an image of war as a force overpowering all its participants is a mystery. Yet following as it does the destruction and depravity piled on the enlisted men, any more havoc experienced by the commanding officers would probably not increase the atmosphere of despair. A decrease is just as possible. Readers may experience satisfaction on seeing General Cummings as perplexed and stymied as Gallagher or Valsen. Prior to Cummings' undoing, nature has been cast as the unpredictable power, whereas the army at least from the enlisted man's viewpoint, has been absolutely predictable. Now at the end, all components in the wartime world represent pure chance or chaos. The credit for winning Anopopei technically belongs to Major Dalleson who "had a way with a cliche" (384). Meanwhile, the absent super-strategist Cummings returns and discovers his tailored campaign resolved independent of his plans. Despite the official verdict recognized by the Pentagon, accrediting his moderate success, he feels strangely thwarted, sensing his personal limitations, with his military and political goals forever beyond his reach. How fate has determined him! At the hierarchical bottom, Croft's soldiers, already more conditioned to a haphazard existence, seem less disturbed by their meaningless mission—"And that pleased them too. The final sustaining ironies" (708). With the common soldiers yearning for the eventual peacetime, the novel ends. But the General dreads the return to normality. Perhaps Mailer's own "final sustaining" hope includes this tomorrow when the ordinary soldiers will be less "dead" as men, while the generals with their diminished power find themselves a little more "naked." Whatever optimism *The Naked and the Dead* contains seems minor when contrasted with its greater stress on portraying mankind, alienated, a slave to anxiety, in a futile existence. From its final vantage point, Mailer's fictional world is still inhabited by atavistic beings. Animalism in various guises still reigns supreme.

In Mailer's second novel, *Barbary Shore*, war has changed from hot to cold, but Mailer's vision of man, imprisoned and isolated, with human dignity going or gone, remains constant. The dramatic area is again restricted. Like the microcosmic island, an insignificant Brooklyn boardinghouse, a little world, functions as a metaphor of the human mind. Its macrocosmic extensions imply that cerebral man is imprisoned inside an establishment honeycombed with distinct corridors and separate rooms, where minds are even more partitioned from each other than are the tenants' bodies. Replacing the wartime gulf between men based on

a military hierarchy is a more subtle ranking of the
various roomers' minds. McLeod's great intellect
seems hopelessly foreign to his wife Guinevere's overdone cliches or his daughter's specialized baby talk.
Outside this family, communication is just as futile.
Hollingsworth, the secret agent trained to interrogate,
usually prefers cloaking his meanings, whereas Mikey
Lovett and Lannie Madison, victims of amnesia and
hallucination respectively, seldom find any understanding ear. Alongside this inability to relate to each
other, the inhabitants confined within the boardinghouse represent an enclosed world wherein every mind
reveals nothing but the rootlessness inherent in the
structure surrounding the thought. Rooms, like values
and attitudes, are rented for brief occupancy. Believers
keep passing through. Ideas shift with the boarder.
Fringing these rented walls are a seascape and landscape offering no more stability than the house itself.
The outside scenes are usually as tainted and blurred
as the intellectuality within. When a human form
appears in the neighborhood, he resembles the other
derelicts peering from the windows: "a bum wandered
up from the Bowery to retch his whiskey into the
water" (120). Inside, the same alienation exists between the tenant and his room. This applies even to
Guinevere, technically the landlady, whose basement
apartment "surprises" Lovett, because her "furniture
was modest, but she had achieved some decent effects" (52). Her own living quarters do not reflect her
tasteless and immodest personality. His wife's otherwise sordid and disorderly premises certainly do not
mirror McLeod's ". . . elements of such order, demanding, monastic" (34). Lovett labels his own room
"an oppressive and sultry hole" (8), while pronounc-
ing the entire house to be "filthy," which does not
harmonize with Guinevere's husband's "mania about
neatness" (20). In Lannie Madison's case, a rear-
ranged sofa "temporarily facing a wall, its back to the
center of the room," made it, like her, "separated

from the rest of the room" (105–6). But the most telling sign of the alienation pervading the boarding-house occurs when Lovett remarks on his arrival: "It was a big house and gave the impression of being an empty house. Downstairs there were ten names arranged in ten brackets next to as many bells which did not ring" (19). Of the ten roomers, Lovett the narrator introduces his readers only to four. In *Barbary Shore*, the spatial figures are as ripe for isolation as those of Mailer's earlier novel.

Another device retained in the second novel is displacement in time. At the very beginning Mailer creates within Mikey Lovett an ability to experience the present with renewed freshness, without the past blurring it with any preconceived notions. Lovett's "enormous present" is supposedly caused by his alleged amnesia. But as novel technique, the narrator's inability to recall the past enables Lovett to recreate the grotesqueness in a world which could be otherwise misconceived, if viewed normally, to be the commonplace world everyone inhabits. In effect, he becomes a consciousness tuned to report out the present in its most authentic sense—"I had no past and was therefore without a future. The blind grow ears, the deaf learn how to see, and I acquired both in compensation; it was natural, even obligatory, that the present should possess the stage" (4–5). Severed from all previous experience, including his own, he is a learner intent on synchronizing events and his perceptions of them. But on his psychic journey through the boardinghouse, he soon learns that others exist in their own temporal plane. Hollingsworth's daily life seems oriented toward the future. Schooled to be an interrogator, to ferret out various secrets, Hollingsworth lives in anticipation, since his personality is being shaped by answers about to be revealed at any time. At the other end of the time circuit stands McLeod. His search for identity depends on how well he can evaluate his past. Through the years the guilt growing out of his perverse misuses of socialistic dogma has increased to where purgation can be achieved only through an enforced confession of his past errors. Once Hollingsworth has helped him perform this task, McLeod can justify his own present existence only through self-destruction.

Immediately before McLeod's suicide, the various temporal dimensions pertaining to these characters converge. McLeod's obsession with a meaningful past soon will be resolved by his fatal acknowledgement of his meaningless present. Inversely, Hollingsworth shifts attention from his future to his past, inasmuch as his mission ends with McLeod's suicide. Skipping out with remnants from McLeod's past, including his wife and daughter, the secret agent no longer concerns himself with present events inside the boardinghouse. Hollingsworth's future is no longer a secret. His success on "Barbary" will be determined by how well he can apply his bestial style. To safeguard against re-adapting to civilization, the new man must always concentrate on his past. The oncoming melodramatic climax has also temporarily reduced Lovett to this state: "I shuddered with terror and undefined sorrow, as unashamedly miserable as a child in the immensity of an empty house" (289). Paradoxically, just when Lovett's preoccupation with the present begins dovetailing with his teacher McLeod's, the lesson ends—McLeod's suicide and Hollingsworth's escape emphasize the present futility, prompting Lovett to focus on the future and his novel (290). At some unforeseeable future time, the narrator will reappraise his past experiences and perhaps complete his "large ambitious work about an immense institution never defined more exactly than that, and about the people who wandered through it" (58).

Another reason why this novel remains so undefined is Lovett's initial judgment: "the story seemed absurd and I was abysmally dejected" (58). The inharmonious events occurring in the "immense institution" are contrary to reason primarily because this microcosmic world is dedicated to barbarism. It is a kind of secular limbo, a world in transit between civilization and the mass of amorality below.

This resembles Mailer's earlier fictional world. Despite the hot war turned cold, the accent is still on "the conflict between the beast and seer in man." The jungle now is modified to fit its peacetime counterpart —a filthy dwelling. Natural storms and typhoons are converted into psychological ones raging inside the characters' minds. Man's imprisonment, in effect, is made less physical and more cerebral. The various inmates no longer fear instant death as much as gradual mental derangement. The "naked" have discarded their uniforms but the "beast" and the "seer" still wage war in civilian clothes. In regard to this thematic likeness in his two novels, Mailer makes no direct comment. Unlike the scattered giveaways on theme which followed *The Naked and the Dead,* Mailer has kept silent about *Barbary Shore,* except for ironic discussions concerning its bad press, and except for this one critical statement.

> Yet, it could be that if my work is alive one hundred years from now, *Barbary Shore* will be considered the richest of my first three novels for it has in its high fevers a kind of insane insight into the psychic mysteries of Stalinists, secret policemen, narcissists, children, Lesbians, hysterics, revolutionaries—it has an air which for me is the air of our time, authority and nihilism stalking one another in the orgiastic hollow of this century. (ADV, 94)

Again the title provides a clue to the book's general theme. Both the terms "shore" and "coast" refer to any lengthwise border or edge, and yet Mailer has significantly preferred the more unexpected "Barbary Shore," since the latter term singles out a boundary adjoining a sea, lake, stream, or any other body of water, whereas "coast" usually refers only to borders of seas. Here Mailer hints at a metaphorical distinc-

tion between two lands and the water in between.
The first shore—the one that man has already begun
to abandon—represents civilization and the solidarity
it gives with its traditional mores. Inversely, the adjoining water impinging on the new land symbolizes
mankind's urge to drift from a hybrid form of bestiality to a pure state of barbarism. Labeling the setting
"Barbary" further suggests that the atavism has already made inroads. The boardinghouse bulges with
unmistakable signs that its inhabitants are reverting to
cruelty, vulgarity and belief in superstition—symptoms of eventual barbarism. In fact, the land seems as
threatening as the water. Since "Barbary" can also
refer to some exotic, pagan or romantic land, the
water may be a symbolic means of transporting irrational man to what he blindly conceives to be a more
desirous and authentic Barbary"—a utopia inverted to
complete the transition from man to brute. The
boardinghouse becomes the point of embarkation.
This is implied when Guinevere and Hollingsworth,
the two clearest embodiments of barbarism in the
novel, plan to flee from the boardinghouse together—
"To the ends of the earth. To Barbary—I like the
sound of that" (205). But Hollingsworth's postpon-
ing the journey to "finish certain of his obligations"
suggests that the new breed of man is not developed
enough to make it as a complete brute. In the final
analysis, mankind in *Barbary Shore* is still poised on
the dividing line between civilization and barbarism.

In Mailer's second novel, there are only six important characters. Unlike *The Naked and the Dead*,
with its numerous characters shaped in realism, the
few here become personified ideas. There is a sextet of
three males and three females, and within the latter
there is an inner triad, one female signifying the
human body, another the mind, another the spirit—
all in a pathological condition.

Guinevere McLeod is the epitome of a sick body.
Possessing an earthy shape, and having a background

in burlesque, she appears to be an incarnation of sensual and sexual fulfillment. This is an illusion because Guinevere prefers either to tantalize or bargain with her physical wares. She is a sex advertiser whose motives are materialistic and vulgar. The resume of her "story that's worth a million bucks" (61) is a perfect example of tasteless or barbaric art. What may have been a wholesome and genuine personality rooted in the physical becomes in Guinevere a warped and sick facsimile of the human body.

Another female in the household is sick in mind. The "mad" in Lannie Madison's name is no accident. A victim of hallucinations caused by disillusionment and guilt, she allows her former idealism to be perverted into a confusion of bad with good. Her masochistic yearnings for Hollingsworth and her Lesbian debasement with Guinevere are both idealized by Lannie into goodness, beauty and love. Of all the characters, Lannie makes the most woeful and futile attempt to recover what normality remains in an otherwise chaotic world.

If any character is pure symbol, it is Monina. Her name alone carries symbolic weight. It suggests that she embodies "Monism," or the belief in a single substance or ultimate reality. Such symbolic naming may explain why Mailer singles out "children" as one of his vital concerns in *Barbary Shore*. Despite being less than four years old, Monina is an adult grotesque —"The child was completely naked . . . her body was extraordinary. She was virtually a miniature of a girl of eighteen, the limbs round, slender curves flowing from shoulder to hip, her luminous blonde hair lovely against the pale flesh" (61). Mailer's linking daughter to mother by stressing their physical and psychological kinship, especially their mutual obsession with sexual vanity, makes Monina's role clearer. At first glance, Monina's manner of speaking—a crude blend of adult ideas and baby talk—may seem like a direct inheritance from the intellectual McLeod. But who is Monina's real father? According to Guinevere: "I'm not saying Monina was born the same way they claim for Jesus, but you know it might have been a similar kind of thing, the doctors are always discovering new secrets, and who's to say?" (68). Of course Guinevere's absurd allusion to the virgin birth springs from a superstitious mind, and yet it still adds an ethereal quality to the child. This is emphasized when Lovett introduces her—"The sunlight illumined her golden hair and steeped her face and arms in a light so intense her flesh appeared translucent . . . I had for a moment the whimsy that she was an angel, perplexed by the mechanics of living" (47).

As Guinevere and Lannie stand for sick body and sick mind respectively, Monina embodies sick spirit. Her characterization is based on the motif of innocence yielding to experience. An omen of the generation soon to be weaned. Monina is a kind of *tabula rasa*, a newcomer to a world whose inhabitants are drifting toward barbarism. What rational power she has fades as she becomes more and more estranged from McLeod's influence. If she has inherited any of her supposed father's intellectual powers, these are being rapidly undermined by her mother. From Guinevere, Monina is receiving an education in vulgarity, which will quicken when the child passes into the new family relationship with Guinevere and Hollingsworth—those future sojourners at "Barbary." As the new world's inheritor, Monina's thematic role reflects her symbolic name. In a sense, she is an orphan, deprived of normal family and environment. Metaphorically, she can also be likened to a contaminated spirit, a future embodiment of "monism" at "Barbary," because the duality between mind and body will soon no longer exist, resulting in the sole reality of instinct and barbarism.

As counterparts to the three females, the three male characters reflect causes rather then effects. The chief reason why bodies, minds and spirits are broken and unsound is that there is no longer any rational foundation to this world.

This spotlights the characterization of McLeod. Formerly a revolutionary hellbent on improving mankind, he has since turned stagnant and inept. His "analytical disposition" though barren, is all that he has left. Analysis has little relevance to his wife, whose moral values are so emotional that McLeod's marriage to Guinevere (his antithesis) becomes a miscarriage of morality. As Lovett sees it: "A moral man, I'm convinced. He wanted to punish himself, so he married her" (76). Feeling an intense guilt toward his past rejection of his grand ideals, McLeod finds his power to believe in the older values constantly waning. Eventually, he realizes he is a living anachronism. His actions are still orderly but his rented dwelling is disorderly. His mind has adjusted to those ideas at the top while his wife's remained geared to the bottom. Ideological alienation expands into the moral and personal, and soon McLeod has "killed the alternatives" (304). The result, suicide. With his passing, so passes the embodiment of love for ideas, and the boardinghouse and the sea outside are left to the present control of the new man.

Barbarism is prefigured in the characterization of Leroy Hollingsworth. Only in his twenties, this secret policeman has no respect for humanism. Instead he has become empty, severed from historical morality and high knowledge, professing only an admiration for his organization. According to his dogma, man's mind should not be so much discarded as modernized: "To be a good man in the organization a knowledge of the psychological is essential" (264). For him, knowledge concerning people is to be standardized and desensitized, to be converted into massive data, gathered through means similar to the Pavlovian allusion in *The Naked and the Dead*. Concepts suggesting imagination or originality are passé. Validity should rather be justified by "facts and not words"

(234). Such a worshipper of spiritless fact must therefore conclude that McLeod ("near-fifty") is an ideological relic. Hollingsworth's immediate mission centers on harassing his victim into giving up a mysterious "little object." His ultimate mission remains—to wipe out McLeod's revolutionary notion that the future belongs to the individuals who envision mankind in an advanced civilized state. As an alternative, Hollingsworth offers this message: "you could still have a good time if you'd realize that everyone is like you, and so it's pointless to work for the future" (269). Eventually some future will come but it will not require any individual effort, only a passive assimilation into an authoritarian world where to destroy provides more success and happiness than to create. He is already having his "good time," being a vicious interrogator, latent homosexual, and petty sadist. Once this prototypal man has completed his mission, he and the new woman, Guinevere, can depart on their journey to "Barbary."

The recorder of this history of mankind wavering between two futures is, of course, Mikey Lovett. Despite being as old as Hollingsworth, he is still a kind of *tabula rasa*. His amnesia heightens his insight into the present situation, transforming his learning process into one resembling Monina's. After his first genuine discussion with McLeod, Lovett tells about its aftereffects: "And with the labor of parturition, a heartland of whole experience was separating itself to float toward the sea. I was an adolescent again" (125). There follows a long reverie. Unlike Monina, a child experiencing the present through past associations, Lovett must mature by returning to adolescence and discarding all past impressions. His education requires him to experience the present without any preconceived notions before he reappraises it. Only then can he construct a future.

The narrator's characterization should therefore provide the key to whether *Barbary Shore* contains any optimism to offset its more obvious pessimism. Mailer has said nothing about his second novel in this respect. His narrator undergoes much learning before deciding where his allegiance belongs. Hollingsworth is labeled "the criminal" while McLeod is called "the moralist" (238). Later the didactic McLeod ends a suicide and Lovett can feel only a minor consolation, noting how the others depart for "Barbary" (307–8). Hollingsworth, realizing his organization will condemn his attempt at absconding with the "little object," is "panicky" and "terrified." "I'm doomed" — shouts Guinevere, passing into the control of her new sadistic mate. Equally damned sounds Monina with her "I want my daddy." And Lovett frames all this psychic mayhem with this significant phrase — "The shrieking and caterwauling of animals washed over the dam." The exodus to "Barbary" has begun. The only legacy from the older shoreline is McLeod's "little object," which is never identified. It probably represents, in the present context, that "heritage" from the civilized state when mankind's ideals were tuned to the aspirations of individuals. McLeod's "little object" eludes Hollingsworth; Lovett receives it. These "remnants" from civilization spark the narrator with enough hope to "work and to study and to keep my eye on the door." But Lovett's optimism seems remote since his present awareness remains directed at "the boat drift(ing) ever closer to shore."

The new way Mailer presents his old theme explains why *Barbary Shore* seems less optimistic than *The Naked and the Dead*. Common to both novels is a microcosmic view of man slipping into a subhuman existence. But the atavism in the first novel is so correlated with wartime that the reader cannot help but expect the return to peacetime will reverse the drift from the "seer" to the "beast." Man has indeed returned to peacetime in *Barbary Shore*, but to no improved fate. No longer outwardly "naked," humanity seems internally "dead," because the new milieu is, down-deep, only a more insidious copy of the old. Switching from the cold to another hot war will only speed the descent to bestiality. Unlike *The Naked and the Dead*, *Barbary Shore*'s rosy overtones reach the reader with much less immediacy. The kind of dramatic action on Anopopei disappears in the Brooklyn boardinghouse. In fact, the latter third of *Barbary Shore* almost reads like a debate. Also, the nondramatic relies on personifications. As realistic characterization decreases, the symbolism in the narrative increases until the whole novel verges on allegory. Even Mailer's use of a first person narrator (with immediacy usually guaranteed) creates no reader empathy, because Lovett is a passive and aloof observer. Despite its omniscient viewpoint and objective tone, *The Naked and the Dead* communicates its message (down to its ironic optimism) with more impact than does the more abstract and airy *Barbary Shore*, with its black theme a result of its blank style.

The Deer Park
America's Lost Cool

Mailer's second novel begins—"Probably I was in the war"—and if the "probably" in Mikey Lovett's very first sentence is Mailer's indirect way of saying—"please do not understand my narrator too quickly" —then his third novel, *The Deer Park*, recasts the former advice into a fervid plea. Prefacing this novel is a quotation from André Gide: "Please do not understand me too quickly." There is a shift from narrator to author. Mailer himself admits this while discussing the careful revisions of the novel, "Because, determined or no that they would read me slowly, praying my readers would read me slowly" (*ADV*, 239). This appeal to readers is no mere advertisement for those changes in style in the revised version. What is more significant is Mailer's specific remark, when adapting the novel into a play, that "the action takes place in Hell" (442). Elsewhere Mailer says: "when I was doing *The Deer Park* as a novel, characters existed on one level. It seemed to me that putting them into Hell deepened the meaning of their moral experience. That the situation of being in Hell and not knowing . . . it is the first dislocation of the moral space" (383). Technically the setting is a Hollywood resort. Still, it is a kind of inverted paradise, despite the inhabitants' inability to recognize it as such. The resort is really a modern counterpart of the historical "Deer Park"—Louis XV's orgiastic playground. Again Mailer's fictional world displays mankind drifting downward into moral blackness, except that now the imprisoned do not see their counterfeit paradise changing into a genuine hell.

Spatially *The Deer Park* is confined for the most part to a Southern California resort called Desert D'Or. Its less elegant name, Desert Door, in the past served notice to miners that this was the gateway to gold. Its later Frenchified name befits its belated aristocrats, whose desert is a metaphor of their own descent into a spiritual and sexual wasteland. As a memorial of its updated name, the architecture is "all new," sleek and artificially modern. Narcissism shapes all interior decoration: "Like living in a room whose walls are mirrors" (3). Paradoxically such an environment reflects none of its perverse purpose to its inmates. One of its acknowledged social leaders, Herman Teppis, views the resort terrain as "A musical. It's full of cowboys and these fellows that live alone, what do you call them, hermits" (74). His romantic ballyhoo (cowboys, hermits and pioneers) of these decadent surroundings is grotesquely humorous, and yet this comic character and his observations indicate his and the others' intense blindness toward their own barren existences. Dorothea O'Faye's home is nicknamed "The Hangover." The coterie gathering there is called the "court," again mirroring the analogy between Desert D'Or's society and Louis XV's aristocracy. In terms of values and goals, this privileged class is wholly dedicated to debasing the emotional life of America.

Men are still imprisoned (just this side of the jungle), but the action in this novel is not confined to a single setting. Unlike the first two novels, *The Deer Park* presents its action with spatial extensions. Always looming in the resort's background is Hollywood, its capital, where a few scenes occur. The narrator, who journeys to Mexico City and New York, also creates a sense of an expanding area of action. Since the action occasionally leaves Desert D'Or, the relationship between microcosm and macrocosm is less

obvious than the earlier novels. Instead the physical
world of *The Deer Park* appears to be intact and
extensive as to need no counterpart. But Sergius
O'Shaugnessy, the narrator, says "two worlds" are in-
terrelated: "There was a real world as I called it, a
world of wars and boxing clubs and children's homes
on back streets, and this real world was a world where
orphans burned orphans. It was better not even to
think of this. I liked the other world in which almost
everybody lived. The imaginary world" (47). By implication, the "real world" remains outside the enclosed park: a world that—when authentically viewed
—is based on the solid verities, each distinct from
another, as joy from pain, desire from cruelty, and
love from sex. Yet the "other world" of Hollywood
make-believe confuses its verities, mistaking one thing
for something else, especially sex for love. Man, in
The Deer Park, is incarcerated in a jungle of self-
deception.

"This is partly a novel of how I felt at the time"
(121)—so states O'Shaugnessy, the narrator whose
movement in point-of-view reveals how Mailer manipulates time to fit his theme. Technically the action is
related in both the first and third persons. The novel
begins in the first person, as O'Shaugnessy presents a
prolonged introduction of himself, the setting and the
characters. Only in Part II does the story begin. Again
O'Shaugnessy remains the key observer, though he
participates less. In the third part the narrator's role in
the action decreases even more—("I have the conceit
that I *know* what happened" [100]). Here he is referring to the Eitel-Esposito affair, which is told in the
third person, although O'Shaugnessy's tone colors
every word. In effect, the point-of-view becomes that
of a mere first-person observer with omniscient
powers, except during his affair with Lulu Meyers,
dramatized in the first person. Later O'Shaugnessy
relies on secondary sources for information and, after
his departure from Desert D'Or, on letters and hear-

say—("I heard from a waitress what had happened to Marion and Elena" [327]). After settling in New York, O'Shaugnessy becomes a sort of visionary observer: "I could always think of Eitel, and I could see his life, and Elena's life, and the life of the capital, until at times my imagination would take me to all the corners I would never visit again, and their life became more real to me than anything of my own and I would see them on the round of their days" (356–57). Then follows a final chapter where the narrator sees into the future and gives final form to the characters through his godlike imagination.

Why does Mailer complicate the point of view? He does so partly to give the impression of people trapped in a hell. Its dimensions are psychological rather than physical. The inhabitants of "the Deer Park" cannot perceive that their imaginations affect the honesty of their actions. Sexual promiscuity and bestial appetites are fancied to be tokens of a human paradise. Surrounded by such self-deception, O'Shaugnessy must never rationalize if he expects to mature with his personal identity and artistic sensibility intact. To get at the roots of the mores at Desert D'Or, at what really motivates its people, may require narration ranging from objective report to subjective vision. When necessary his imagination must see through illusory actions, sifting truth from sham. Contrasted with the narrator (and also Marion Faye) are those whose imaginations are a vehicle for personal fantasy, that results in rationalization and self-deception. Though they may consider themselves part of an aristocracy, these Hollywood personalities are nothing but sophisticated counterparts of Hollingsworth and others ready to embark to "Barbary."

Since hell is usually associated with darkness, so is Desert D'Or: "One seemed to leave the theatrical darkness of afternoon for the illumination of night, and the sun of Desert D'Or became like the stranger who the drunk imagines to be following him" (4).

Here the residents escape to bars and parties, shunning the daylight. Like the darkened movie theatre, Desert D'Or also represents the nighttime of the human soul. Lottie Munshin, the wife of Collie (an interesting name, in this present context) and the daughter of Herman Teppis, offers this comment concerning time: "people should follow the same hours animals do, and they would have the natural health of an animal" (77). Her obsessive hobby, breeding dogs, underlines Mailer's preoccupation with a world where sensation is out of joint—another style of man reverting to beast. The structure also contains echoes of *Barbary Shore*. Again spatial and temporal dimensions are correlated. O'Shaugnessy remarks of Desert D'Or's architecture: "everything is in the present tense" (2). But like Mikey Lovett, only O'Shaughnessy and Marrion Faye understand how this society has adjusted to the present, whereas Eitel and the other inmates view their present in terms of past or future. If the narrative clocks are synchronized to different time patterns in *The Deer Park*, this is Mailer's way of portraying how artificial his fictional world is. It is a never-never land, no more real than the movies. If that time ever comes when Hollywood's ideal is mistaken for the norm of reality, man's imprisonment in a psychological hell (where the genuine and the sham are indistinguishable) will be complete.

The two earlier themes—the "conflict of the seer and the beast," and mankind's drift towards barbarism—still haunt Mailer's third novel, despite its many overly sophisticated and decadent characters. The choice of title again provides a key to the book's ultimate meaning. As its preface informs: the "Deer Park" was the royal reservation set aside by the French King Louis XV for sexual orgies. In the twentieth century, such sex no longer has the justification of royal prerogative, and a new rationalization for extravagant sexual behavior must be invented. One source is Hollywood, with its "sentimental cheats of the movie

screen" (*ADV*, 23). There, sex and love are inseparable emotions, and so the residents of the modern
"Deer Park" fail to see any difference between their
noble intentions and their promiscuous behavior.
Their physical corruption mirrors their mental and
spiritual decay.

The most complete spokesman for these hypocrites
is Herman Teppis. Nearly all his words take on misplaced values. In chapter 20, one of the most humorous parts of the book, he tries to pair off Lulu Meyers
and Teddy Pope, whose eccentric sex lives are noto-
rious. Teppis never admits that he is trying to capitalize on publicity. Instead he speaks of "sincere love"
and "Motherhood"—all the products of "the big family right here at Supreme Pictures" (265). Yet a rare
sincerity takes place at the end of the chapter. After
Teppis has cajoled a call-girl into performing *fellatio*,
he rationalizes: " 'There's a monster in the human
heart,' he said aloud to the empty room. And to
himself he whispered, like a bitter old woman, close to
tears, 'They deserve it, they deserve every last thing
that they get.' " (285). On the other hand, Dorothea
O'Faye, Elena Esposito, Lulu Meyers, Collie Munshin, Tony Tanner and Teddy Pope all share Teppis'
illusion that sex must have an ennobling emotion.

Of the characters kept in this park, Charles Francis
Eitel represents the most intense struggle to escape its
confines. Not only does he tell (as his name, pro-
nounced "eye-TELL," suggests) about his capitula-
tion as an artist to superior political and aesthetic
powers, he also tells about his social and sexual predic-
aments. Originally classified with the emigres, Eitel
unconsciously desires full restoration to his former
high rank within the group. For a while he wavers
between outer integrity and inner security. This inde-
cision is resolved through his affair with Elena, which,
despite all the commotion about love and want and
need, is ultimately reduced to this "conclusion":
"Why should a second-rate man spend so much time

on a fifth-rate woman? It was not logical. Second-rate
men sought out second-rate women; the summits of
society were inhabited by such people, and why had
he deserted his caste?" (204). His very name—
Charles Francis Eitel—echoes a bygone, almost Vic-
torian, concern with protocol and caste, and Marion
Faye, the most perceptive dweller in the park, agrees:
". . . so middle-class. Very nineteenth century, you
know" (23). The last century's vestiges within Eitel
clash with Hollywood's sexual morality and become
scrambled to a surface concern with sex as "technique" or "style." Nor is it surprising that he is the
best player at charades at Hollywood parties (242),
since he constantly plays at "who am I" with both
himself and women in the bedroom. At certain times,
his mode of rationalization veers toward momentary
honesty. While admitting how he prostituted his art
to commercialism, he says: "In the end that's the only
kind of self-respect you have. To be able to say to
yourself that you're disgusting" (306). But such con-
fessionals are brief, and otherwise he lapses into a
twilight world with Elena, becoming nearly "first-
rate" while his wife climbs steadily from third to
second. Before his readmission to the deer park, Eitel,
according to Marion Faye, is a "frustrated teacher"—
"Deep-down a John like Eitel is always obsessed with
wanting people to trust him" (338).

His most willing pupil, who almost "trust(ed)
him," is O'Shaugnessy. Apart from his roles as narrator and artist, he takes on the style of Mikey Lovett—
another Mailer youth growing up in a world whose
values are disintegrating. War is again seen in its
aftermath. But unlike *Barbary Shore*, the cold war,
except for O'Shaugnessy's occasional reveries, stays far
in the background, and it hardly ever intrudes on
the "enormous present" in the "park." Outside its
confines, the war serves another purpose. Memories of
physical mutilation and violence provide the narrator
(and incidentally the reader) with a yardstick from

the past to measure the emotional mutilation and violence waged in the present swank surroundings. O'Shaugnessy is intentionally camouflaged to appear as the Hollywood prototype: "six-feet one," blond, husky and "good-looking." But immediately he warns the reader: "When I would put on my uniform, I would feel like an unemployed actor who tries to interest a casting director by dressing for the role" (5). This is exactly what he remains: an actor or poser whose choice whether to accept or reject Desert D'Or's standards is made through his gradual awareness that his own human substance is so different that it can never be compatible. Although Eitel labels him "a twentieth-century gentleman" (34), Sergius earlier has told the reader his true origins: "When I was twelve, I found out my last name was not O'Shaugnessy but something which sounded close in Slovene. It turned out the old man was mongrel sailor blood—Welsh-English from his mother, Russian and Slovene from his father, and all of it low. There is nothing in the world like being a false Irishman" (20). From the very outset his temperament is out of joint at the Hollywood playground, where everyone blindly agrees that self-deception is the ticket for entering its society. Unlike the others, Sergius recognizes his own falseness. This enables him to experience the sexual wasteland without deluding himself, and he escapes with his integrity as man and artist intact, but only after realizing how hypocritical Lulu and the others are, how inept the wavering Eitel is, and how honest and adept Marion Faye remains.

If the "Deer Park" needs a caretaker, the super-candidate is Faye. Stationed at its center, armed with the necessary credentials—his father being a real prince and his mother reigning supreme at "The Hangover" —he deliberately renounces his birthright. Instead he decides to satiate himself by experiencing Desert D'Or and its sick sex with honesty. To the problem: is this society morally guilty or are its individuals?—

Faye would find the very question absurd. It is not a question of his mother's world lacking any higher values; rather, the problem revolves around this world's inability to label the lewd, "lewd." Experiencing immorality without illusion shuts out personal pretense. Reversing the narrator's behavior—the adding of "O" to Shaugnessy to advertise a princely air—Faye drops his "O". Still, the remnant of his name, consciously retained, brims with significance. "Marion," sounding like the feminine name, hints at his bisexuality and his kinship with characters like Teddy Pope and Elena Esposito. His last name, Faye, is close to "fay" or "ofay," a Negro term for a white person. A certain transfusion of values from the Negro world at the social bottom—picking up a knack at prostitution, violence, and drug addiction and other underworld staples—enables Marion Faye to increase his power in a corrupt world surfaced with social finery. At Desert D'Or, Marion's initials reflect the loss of specific sex roles—Male or Female. Befitting his name, his awareness of the sexual condition of men and women alike seems so thorough that he is almost able to predict the outcome of relationships based on pathological sex. In this connection, Faye's early desire to be a priest (328) accents the motif of inverse religion existing at Desert D'Or. Eventually he stands in the pit, seeing and naming all. Don Beda, one of the arch satyrs, admits Faye's superiority: "You know . . . people like you give a bad name to people like me" (336). In a world taken over by bestial man, Marion Faye has become its seer.

Teddy Pope, Collie Munshin and Jay-Jay are lesser prelates in the hierarchy. They all link their private romances to the Bimmler rating, the public pulse of status and success. The way Eitel bastardizes his original art script is the "way of the world" at Desert D'Or, and shows how these various resort dwellers degenerate with one another. The title of the completed movie—"Saints and Lovers"—displays another "final sustaining irony." Both on and off the screen, these people become sensually entangled with each other in a calloused manner, and yet sanction their acts and thoughts by investing them with a veneer of sanctity. And like the original Eitel hero, "(their) sainthood (is) remembered only by the despairing round of (their) sins" (127). Only O'Shaugnessy escapes the "Park" and this indictment, and only Marion Faye possesses the courage to remain and affirm it.

The Deer Park is a highly moralistic novel. It criticizes the sham and insincerity that shape the bedroom mores of Hollywood. Despite its glamor, prestige and romance, Hollywood sex is really sordid and obscene. Undoubtedly Mailer feels concerned that critics or reviewers reversed the book's intention after a quick reading, with their responses (conditioned by cinema romance) far too pat. Such readers may find in this third novel further proof of Mailer's so-called sexual preoccupation and his boyish plan to do away with all sexual inhibitions. Actually the novel does not ridicule sexual inhibition so much as insist that it be applied in an authentic manner. Once hypocrisy is exposed and ousted, physical desire may become wholesome and produce relationships wherein the partners can mutually grow. In his introductory epigraph from André Gide, Mailer, besides asking his readers to "understand his real purpose, also warns them of preconceived notions which may blur what his theme intends to do. But even "understanding" readers may read too slowly, and Mailer cannot afford to be understood too quickly. The label "didactic" may be too much for any contemporary novel to bear, since readers shy away from open preaching. To safeguard himself against the occasional slow but understanding reader who may resent a cheap sermon, Mailer uses various tricks of technique and style to diminish the look of moralizing. Most of the plot is interspersed with humor, sometimes bitingly grotesque, at other times merely funny. Comic characters like Herman

Teppis and Collie Munshin often unconsciously mouth their own condemnation, ready-made puppets of the satiric author. For the most part, the dialogue —sleek, pert and seasoned with Hollywood idiom ("don't panic love bucket")—also aids in creating a casual tone. Mailer's complex point-of-view also contributes. Enough distance must be maintained between author and narrator, and between narrator and story, to make certain that the moral message is as understated as possible. In this way, neither Mailer nor O'Shaugnessy can be labled the judge of the fictional world. In *The Deer Park*, Mailer's technique and style offer his readers a blackout of morality, but not enough to blot out the message that Hollywood sex turns America into a jungle of sick minds without a happy ending.

8

An American Dream
The Singular Nightmare

New directions, even in Mailer's fiction—"*An American Dream* is a departure from practically anything I have done before." (*SI*)—contain vestiges of the old, and Mailer's fourth novel can be read (as most critics and reviewers have done) as sardonic social criticism. National ideals seem under attack, as New York, Jack Kennedy, Las Vegas, Marilyn Monroe impart a satiric tone to Rojack's dream. Just before his encounter with Barney Oswald Kelly, the current tycoon, Rojack enters the Waldorf and sees "a nineteenth-century clock, eight feet high with a bas relief of faces: Franklin, Jackson, Lincoln, Cleveland, Washington, Grant, Harrison, and Victoria; 1888 the year" (207). At such times, the theme of national dream turned nightmare seems as obvious as the title suggests. It instead is an outgrowth of Mailer's great admiration of Dreiser's *An American Tragedy* which represents (in Mailer's words) an "end of a period" or "a way of looking at things." If rewritten for the contemporary milieu, Dreiser's book would "no longer be a tragedy; it would be a dream," because in the last forty years, there has been a "transition in consciousness in the character of our times" which has "moved us from the state of the tragedy to the state of the dream" (*SI*). Here Mailer is paraphrasing an earlier idea: "there is a subterranean river of untapped, ferocious, lonely and romantic desires, that concentration of ecstasy and violence which is the dream life of the nation" (*PP*, 38).

Mailer's *An American Dream* does not focus on the

gross Dream of an America crisscrossed with telephone wires and television antennas, whose fad of the
Sixties is the conquest of the moon. Rather Mailer's
novel, based on total cultural delicacies, is a dramatic
critique on those nuances underlining the ambiguous
values in contemporary America, on those individual
roots of American aspirations and ideals. And what
results are peculiar inversions—for does not every
American male, lulled by mass media sex and violence, secretly wish to commit incest or murder his
wife? Such individual fantasies become nightmares
when interpreted by the cultural norm. For Mailer,
the collective ideal is a civilized composite of everyone's primitive desires. The American Dream becomes another cultural mode of regimenting the individual, of rarefying and stultifying his true nature. To
exist in one's own dream world is to avoid having
one's ideals institutionalized. Mailer's fourth novel
isolates one such dream. As his protagonist acts out
his dream, the reader can see what stuff American
dreams are made of—all the magic of murder and sex
and a one-way trip to the moon.

Apart from its implied social criticism, Mailer's latest novel (his first in ten years) reveals new directions
in his fiction. Replacing the use of the microcosm in
his first three novels is the serial structure. Originally
appearing in eight installments in *Esquire*, *An American Dream* is organized through a series of small
crises, but unlike those based on action with an emotional climax ending each episode. More experimen-
tal, Mailer's latest work is a philosophical novel in
serial form and what determines the shape of each
episode is the existential possibilities underlining the
plot. Supplementary to such a plot are the many coincidences that significantly interlock the various characters, as if Rojack's dream were timed by the magic
of events. Since action and character may seem too
unbelievable, Mailer counters fantastic content with a
realistic presentation. The extraordinary must seem

ordinary. Point-of-view is simplified. This is Mailer's first novel with a unified sensibility, as Rojack relates all from his immediate present. His account is remarkably lucid and coherent despite his verging on insanity. Throughout, Rojack narrates with an existential eye which gives equal time to the abnormal and the commonplace. The novel's setting also contributes to Mailer's blend of dream and reality. In the midst of the mythic atmosphere stands New York, as real as a guided tour. Local color excels. Streets, buildings, the idiom all establish a mood of New York. The time is March, nature's time for positive change, a season to match the delicate transition between growth and decay in the protagonist. The handling of time is also less complex in Mailer's latest novel. Here there are no "Time Machines," hazy reveries or future visions. Thirty-two hours of Rojack's life are related in an intense chronological manner. Mailer also manipulates time in its larger aspects. Framing his novel, especially at its beginning, are various historical figures (Jack Kennedy, Mrs. Roosevelt, Henry Wallace, Glen Taylor)—allusions that soon disappear and thereby magnify the isolated and intimate nature of Rojack's one-man history.

The principle that governs Rojack's thirty-two hour history is also the thesis of his university teaching—"Magic, dread and perceptions of death as the center of motivation" (143–44). Or, as developed in a lecture: *On The Primitive View of Mystery:*

> To the savage, dread was the natural result of any invasion of the supernatural: if man wished to steal the secrets of the gods, it was only to be supposed that the gods would defend themselves and destroy whichever man came too close. By this logic, civilization is the successful if imperfect theft of some cluster of these secrets, and the price we have paid is to accelerate our private sense of some enormous if not quite definable disaster which awaits us (159).

Rojack's greatest "theft" or the novel's central act is the murder of his wife. And the "price" Rojack "paid" provides the basis for the novel's plot. But this is not a "Crime and Punishment" novel in the usual sense. As his crime pertains to the institutional modes of retributive law, Rojack goes completely unpunished; the "not quite definable disaster" that punishes has no meaning outside the self. Dread is an internal condition that Rojack can only experience when alienated from everything but the reality of his dream. Basic to his dream vision is "an instinctive belief" that the gods may judge a murderer as an usurper of their power over life and death. To murder is to play god, which stirs up established gods. "And I at this moment was buried in fear. No, men were afraid of murder, but not from a terror of justice so much as the knowledge that a killer attracted the attention of the gods; then your mind was not your own, your anxiety ceased to be neurotic, your dread was real" (204). Rojack's "dream" tells of a mode of crime and a form of punishment known only to Rojack and his creator.

Otherwise, Mailer is as predictably unpredictable as ever. The way magic, dread and death are perceived so thoroughly commits Rojack to an encounter with the "cultural abyss" (murder, suicide, incest, cannibalism) that his experience should be more nightmare than dream. And yet, the novel's ultimate effect is equally fanciful and horrible. These contrary moods are dual products of Rojack's psychology. When he totally internalizes (during his murder of his wife and his walk around the parapet) he communicates a strong and direct sense of fear and dread, but when he shifts his consciousness to the outer world, the intensity slackens and the mood lightens. The world always impinging on Rojack's nightmare is grounded in a kind of magic which is markedly simple, almost naive. It includes patchwork allusions to superstitions, curses, the magic number three, animistic birds, and evil eyes—and other manifestations that belong in any primer on magic. Such unsophisticated and light modes of magic strongly contrast the complex and dark workings of Rojack's mind. What results is a dual mood. Every serious, near-tragic moment in Rojack's experience is complemented by one that is light, near-comic. The latter takes place when Rojack fully exposes himself to the mood of magic without dread, as in his relationship with Cherry. It begins and develops in an atmosphere of gaiety and happiness. Wit and imagination enchant them. Eventually, their affair is consummated on the side of the "silver witch" through the magic of rapport. Despite Rojack's flashes of dread and Cherry's spells of pensiveness, what dominates their relationship is their mutual spontaneity and empathy that creates an interlude of artless happiness. Even at the tragic end, during Cherry's death scene, their mutual understatement in place of the sentimental goodbye implies that their past cannot be erased in time. Of this relationship, the impression that Rojack (and the reader) retains is colored by a magic which transcends the American "plague" with its purity and simplicity. For once, white magic has outlasted the black, and Rojack's affair with Cherry remains more dream than nightmare. But elsewhere in Rojack's experience, magic constantly veers between black and white, as if the worlds of experience and innocence are in deadlocked conflict.

This is most clearly dramatized in the meeting between Rojack and Deirdre, his step-daughter. It occurs just before Rojack's encounter with ultimate evil in the form of Barney Kelly. But first, Rojack must isolate himself with pure innocence and his whole scene with Deirdre represents an idyllic pause in his nightmare, a glimpse of paradise in order to understand the descent to hell. Like Monina in *Barbary Shore*, Deirdre is a child paradox. At twelve, she is another untarnished angel existing in a sordid, materialistic world. Educated in an European convent, she gives off a spiritual aura, speaking in a "disembodied" voice, an echo of a nun. She remains alienated from her "Mummy's" awful bitchiness and Grandfather Kelly's two hundred million dollars worth of callousness. This is reflected in her steadfast sympathy and affection for her step-father. Rojack, on meeting her, feels "suddenly happy"; he is impressed with her sincere grief, is touched when she expresses her loneliness and affection through her desire to stay with him after "Mummy's" funeral. In one sense, Deirdre appears in Rojack's dream as an agent of innocence and purity. But, like Monina, she is also an adult grotesque. Though untarnished by materialism, she is certainly touched with magic—"She was nothing but eyes" (211)—a haunting reminder: like mother, like daughter. Because "she always spoke like an adult" (212), Deirdre fascinates and puzzles Rojack with her blend of eerie superstitions and mystical revelations—that Deborah is not yet dead because she hinted that she belongs to a species of beasts "which stays alive three days after they die" (214). Rojack suddenly feels dread encroach on his happiness. Then just as suddenly he marvels at this twelve year old's wisdom in regard to him and Cherry: "People want to make love after a death" (215). Besides her insight into the mysteries of sex and death, she has a flair for impressionistic verse ("And share my fools for bread"). Such versatility and novelty in adult thought and feeling clearly mark Deirdre as a vital force in Rojack's dream—the possibilities of sharing extremes in mood beyond ordinary experience in time. Rojack hints as much, when he puts her in bed: "She was a child again" (214). Part-adult part-child, Deirdre exists in a superstitious void between womanhood and childhood, and thereby enables Rojack to sense all the nuances between joyful innocence and sorrowful experience. Her very name—made famous by the legendary Irish princess, who out of sorrow for her slain lover committed suicide—suggests she is cursed by her mother's incest, the embodiment of future sorrow. Yet, the quality of present sorrow is made tender to the highest degree. In the entire Mailer canon there is nothing to compare with the following: "A cloud of sorrow concentrated itself into a tear, one pure tear which passed on the mood from her narrow chest into mine. I was in love with Cherry again. 'Bless you, pet,' I said, and then to my surprise I began to cry. I cried for Deborah for a little while, and Deirdre cried with me" (215). Sorrow momentarily relaxes and lulls Rojack, a state of mind immediately dispelled by the anxiety during his violent encounter with Kelly. Within minutes, Rojack must make his sensations match any extreme in mood. Mailer (in depicting Rojack's farewell to Deirdre) has never been so close to sentimentality, and Rojack (in sharing Deirdre's need to be loved) has never been so close to innocence. Even a murderer can sense his time to create if he loses himself in the magic of mood.

Apart from accommodating Rojack to mood, Mailer is also manipulating the mood between himself and his readers. His guiding principle is borrowed from Marx—"quantity changes quality"—which Mailer terms "my favorite remark in all the world" (*SI*). Marx's concept provides the basis of Mailer's conscious attempt to blend two historical milieus. At first, the quality of Rojack's experience seems rooted in modern America. Names ("Jack Kennedy"), dates (November, 1946) and places (Alexandria, Virginia) abound, until a restricted sense of time and space seems assured. Then Rojack introduces the atmosphere of his dream (internal fancy mixed with dread) and as Rojack's oblique visions pervade the action, modern America gradually takes on medieval characteristics.

Rojack's dream-vision, the core of the novel, seems like a modern counterpart of the dream-allegory, a conventional type of medieval literature. The characters, as metamorphosized by Rojack, resemble a medieval bestiary. There is Deborah and her "scent of the

carnivore in a zoo" (30), and Shago Martin whose
"wind" is like "a poisonous snake of mood" (183) —a
gallery of humans transformed into beasts, a kind of
modern beast-epic. Even the hierarchal structure is a
curious blend of the modern and medieval. In addi-
tion to the modern criteria of wealth and power, the
medieval yardstick of good and evil is used as an index
to hierarchy. But according to Rojack's interpretation,
the medieval concept of good at the top extending
down to evil at the bottom is reversed. Evil, in modern America, resides at the top (Kelly, Ganucci, Deborah), and the hierarchy extends down to those who
are relatively good though powerless (Roberts,
Cherry, Deirdre). The medieval also marks Kelly's
history. On Kelly's door, Rojack finds "a medallion
beneath the knocker . . . a lion rampant; 2, 3, sable,
serpent argent . . . And the motto: *Victoria in Caelo
Terraque*" (209). Such traditional allusions (lion, serpent, motto) to Satan transfigure a modern tycoon
into a medieval Beelzebub, and Rojack's literal ascent
to the Waldorf Towers is also a figurative descent to a
kind of Dantean hell—another example of Mailer's
use of the Age of Faith in opposition to the current
faith in power and wealth. Eternal verities (so black
and white in the medieval vision) are now a tentative
grey, a moral relativity so profound that only a dream-
vision can begin to comprehend it. Another way
Mailer submerges modern America in the medieval
milieu is through superstition. Almost every character, despite a surface sophistication, is obsessed with
superstition. Older modes associated with Catholicism (the Irish Kelly's, the Italian Mangaravidis')
predominate; the unknown terrifies and omens in-
trigue Mailer's New Yorkers as if Rojack's dream had
resurrected medieval minds. Even Rojack's acute
sense of psychic smell (which reveal to him the condition of the body and the state of the minds of the
others) can be construed as Mailer's up-dating the
medieval theory of body humours. As for topography:

Rome, the center of the medieval world, has its counterpart in New York, the center of modern America.
But the idea of an Eternal City is but a vestige in the
American imagination; now the best to be had is a
"heavenly city" offered by a murderer. Rojack, like
Dante, also wishes to glimpse the other-world; numerous times he refers to a "heavenly city"—a vision first
taking shape when he pauses at the threshold of murder: "heaven was there, some quiver of jeweled cities
shining in the glow of a tropic dusk" (31). Or later,
after a sex climax with Ruta, he has "a vision immediately after of a huge city in the desert, in some desert,
was it a place on the moon?" (46). This question is
answered in the Epilogue—"The Harbors of the
Moon Again"—because Rojack pauses at Las Vegas,
where magic and dread are reduced to a roll of the
dice and a spin of the wheel. With its incongruous
atmospheres—"the sun at one hundred and two" and
"the seventy degrees of air-conditioned oxygen"
(268)—Las Vegas seems like a transplanted bottom
of Dantian hell with its dual punishment of heat and
cold. Rojack's dream concludes with the knowledge
that what passes for paradise in America is really hell.

Making Las Vegas Rojack's temporary "harbor" is
Mailer's ironic footnote to a crime without any ultimate reward or punishment. At best, Rojack must
salvage those possibilities of judging himself by seeking more authentic expressions of magic and dread in
jungles outside America. The novel ends with Rojack's dream incomplete. To have completed it would
have resulted in Mailer's blending still another milieu
with the modern and medieval—that of the primitive.
A dream's original quality—America of the early
1960's—has long since given way to the quantity of
Rojack's vision which exists outside ordinary space
and time. Mailer's use of the Marxian "quantity
changes quality" makes Rojack's dream so singular
that it becomes universal.

Marx's concept also helps determine Mailer's role

as the writer of *An American Dream*. One quality that a reader would normally expect from a novel is a cause and effect relationship (no matter how complex) in regard to theme, characterization, action and mood. But Mailer, talking about *An American Dream*, maintains that—"I wanted to write a novel of action, of suspense, of character, of manners against a violent background . . . any intellectual aspects of *An American Dream* will have to be dredged up by the critics" (*SI*). At first glance, Mailer's statements make his novel an open secret, not to mention a secret to success, because few readers and critics would expect a nonintellectual book by an arch-intellectual like Mailer. But exactly how "open" is Mailer's stance as novelist who plays down intellect, especially after an energetic ten years with the essay. *An American Dream* may be not a novel of statement (as in the essay) but it is nevertheless filled with implication by image. Intellectual substance is replaced by a kind of intellectual shadow-boxing, on Mailer's part, in the form of a maze of suggestiveness—recurring objects, situations and actions that tantalize with a significance that is seldom clarified. Apparent symbols are not what they seem, as effects appear to exist without causes. Examples are numerous. Throughout, Rojack directs his attention to body extremities. On his first suicidal gesture on the balcony, he is "able better to breathe with one toe pointing at the moon" (12)—and toes and fingers continue to be featured in Rojack's dream apparently to reflect (among other things) the extremity in his actions. There is also an abundance of bird imagery, from bats to canaries, but its exact symbolic meaning (spiritualization or supernatural aid and / or flights of fancy?) never crystallizes. Even more mystifying are those allusions to sex and scatology, as sperm and bowel movements vie to be the greater mystery in Rojack's dream. A reader cannot be expected to comprehend much more than the narrator. And this is Mailer's intention—much will be implied, little will be substantiated. *An American Dream*, with its tantalizing cluster of images, metaphors and near-symbols, is a novel of suggestion, not explanation, a trap for any critic or reader on a symbol hunt. This new direction in Mailer's fiction may have been prompted by the serial structure imposed on him. Pressing deadlines will not be met, especially if a novel is given a studied, systematic presentation. Instead, why not let the quantity of magic (in a novel about magic) change the quality of both the writer and his fiction? If magic is the art of producing effects in the absence of causes, then why not become the novelist as magician who writes a book filled with effects without any causes. Mailer's strategy is, at least, functional since his novel about magic is also based on the aesthetics of magic.

American literary history is a source for still another one of Mailer's new directions—"*An American Dream* in a funny way becomes a novel of manners" (*SI*). As a literary critic, Mailer has elsewhere commented on the traditional role of the novel of manners in American literature. In opposition to the Dreiser school ("whose roots were found in poverty, industrial society, and the emergence of new class") is a "genteel literature which had little to do with power or the secrets of power. They encouraged a literature about courtship and marriage and love and play and devotion and piety and style, a literature which had to do finally with the *excellence* of belonging to their own genteel tradition" (*CC*, 96). *An American Dream*, as a novel of manners, hardly fits such a definition. Undoubtedly, Mailer's qualifying phrase ("in a funny way") implies that he has attempted a new direction—combining the novel of manners with the novel of violence. To accomplish this, the finesse of the drawing room and the know-how of the underworld must have equal value in order to avoid the norms of social behavior. Or, as Mailer describes it: "murder brings out extremes in people, brings out extremes in their manners," and when manners "are pushed to their extreme," they become "more artful and elaborate" (SI).

In the novel, Rojack must learn how to manipulate manners at their most extreme. His survival, as a murder suspect, depends on whether he can alternate, according to the situation, between being polite and being politic. The central image that demonstrates Rojack's external manners is the telephone. Most of Chapter 5—"A Catenary of Manners"—concerns Rojack's "artful" responses to a series of telephone calls from Arthur (the producer of his television show), Dr. Tharchman (his department head at the university), and Gigot (Deborah's zaney and superstitious friend). Besides giving Mailer (through Rojack) the opportunity to satirize the hypocrisy of the mass-media, the smugness of the academy, and the silliness of the wealthy, these telephone conversations also represent Rojack's ordeal in the world of external manners. His behavior must reinforce society's one-sided view of crime and punishment with its oversimplified truth: moderation is impossible in a murderer. This is the stuff of the many moods that Rojack encounters. When he makes his extreme thoughts and acts by a show of moderation, he must remember that (in Mailer's words) "all manners consist of is not breaking the mood" (SI). In attempting this, Rojack exercises much versatility in his reactions to the moods of others. The cat-and-mouse episodes between Roberts (the genteel Irish cop) and Rojack hinge on each man's ability to understand and respect the other's mood. Roberts pursues with psychological kindness and Rojack responds with tactics to avoid capture, though preferably without the other suffering any loss of face. This genial cops-and-robbers continues to the end. When Cherry's death makes him feel sad and frustrated, Rojack appreciates Roberts' stubborn refusal to "break" the mood—"The Irish are the only men who know how to cry for the dirty polluted blood of all the world" (264). Such rapport with manners is rare; usually, other people "break" Rojack's mood and survival depends on his not breaking theirs. The manners of a murderer must be supremely "artful." Rojack's most intense competitor in the art of manners is Kelly who "had two separate manners, one, British; the other, American; you had to learn to distinguish. The British was clipped, jolly, full of tycoon; he might have you knifed but dependably you would receive a full twinkle as the order went down. The American was hard in the eyes" (219). Kelly begins a game, a tension of manners. His British manner seems conciliatory when he asks Rojack to attend Deborah's funeral because "it doesn't matter what is done in private. What is important is the public show—it must be flawless. Because public show is the language we use to tell our friends and enemies that we still have order enough to make a good display" (233). When Rojack refuses ("I really don't care what people say"), Kelly decides to "'push' manners to their extreme. The mood intensifies; it approaches madness, as Kelly matches Rojack's fascination with murder and suicide with his own obsession with incest and orgy. Finally Kelly projects the extreme in his American manner and dares Rojack to join him and Ruta in an orgy.

Kelly's strategy ("shall we get shitty" [254]) makes present manners "elaborate" enough to bring the novel to a climax in regard to external manners. But the nature of the denouement reflects Mailer's real emphasis—a study of manners internalized.

A more intricate and significant "catenary of manners" exists in Rojack's consciousness, a network of inner responses much more complex than his reactions to external stimuli. The quantity of outside manifestations of magic and dread interfere with Rojack's attempts to preserve the quality of his own obsession with murder and suicide. Self-deception (to place greater value outside the individual) must never take

the place of self-knowledge. Salvation (or grace) remains an inner condition, as long as the nature of
guilt is identified as a cultural concept harmful to the
individual. In Rojack's case, possible damnation is
two-fold: social or to give in to guilt; personal or to
give in to insanity. Since the latter is more crucial to
Rojack, the polarity of sanity and insanity is what
supports the "catenary" in his mind. Private manners
become the means of keeping self-control and thereby
remaining sane. Kelly's invitation to an orgy (to make
public the extreme private) tempts Rojack to sample
another equally "artful" set of manners. But Rojack
senses that Kelly's manners, which fit a tycoon in
search of power, place equal value on "public show"
and private actions. Murder, not incest, remains Rojack's index to extreme manners that stress the private
at the expense of the public. To remain lucid on his
own terms, Rojack can only counteract Kelly's temptation (acting out another taboo in order to combat
the fear of public exposure) by exposing himself to his
"elaborate" fear of death; and, he tempts suicide and
"strolls" around the parapet, and invites Kelly (in
order not to "break" the mood) to be a one-man
public, to bear witness ("like a chaplain accompany-
ing a prisoner" [256]) to a private execution or salvation.

It is a qualified salvation according to the novel's
denouement which Mailer contends "if manners
would have been somewhat different, the denouement
would not have occurred" (SI). It does, outside of Las
Vegas in the desert, "by the side of the empty road, a
telephone booth with a rusty dial. Went in and rang
up and asked to speak to Cherry. And in the moon-
light, a voice came back, a lovely voice, and said,
'Why, hello, hon, I thought you'd never call. It's kind
of cool right now, and the girls are swell. Marilyn says
to say hello'" (269–70). As the novel ends, Rojack is
an expert in private manners, which has also caused
Cherry's death, if the magic "voice" he hears on the

parapet is to be believed—"The first trip was done for you, but the second was for Cherry" (261). Moments earlier, when Rojack admits that one trip around the parapet is his limit ("I've lain with madness long enough" [260]), he acknowledges how his over-dependence on internal manners has alienated him from concerns and values outside the self. He has achieved self-control and self-realization but his price is singularity in America. Murder is too intimate an act. Survival, through manners, is just as intimate. Only Rojack knows its basic strategy—adherence to a code of relative manners. He is an "artful" Machiavellian except in one respect. No matter how much the outside world pressures with pain and fear, he must always be harder on himself. Rojack's dream is a psychic-drama of a murderer undergoing more pain and fear than his society can devise. As symbols of his own judge and jury, Rojack's manners become so "elaborate" that he can only relate to the supernatural. At the end, he still has enough rapport with magic to make a person-to-person call to an imaginary heaven on the moon.

Symbolic telephone calls extend throughout Rojack's dream. The "catenary" appears early: "So I went into an outdoor booth, and shivering in the trapped cold air, I phoned her apartment. She was home" (19). At the beginning, Rojack's phone call to Deborah results in murder, an extreme physical act to show the possibilities of damnation or exposure inherent in external manners. At the end, Rojack's phone call to Cherry (not "in the trapped cold air" but in desert heat) results in freedom, an extreme spiritual act to show the possibilities of salvation or survival inherent in internal manners. "In a funny way," *An American Dream* is a novel of manners in which a morality of murder is internalized. Rojack can not be confused with the American Adam in a drawingroom; but, at least, he can be confused with the American Cain escaping detection all the way from New York to Las Vegas. In either case, Rojack's higher quest (his "secret frightened romance with the phases of the moon" [7]) between nightmare and dream will continue. *An American Dream*'s real denouement will occur far out of America, somewhere between the moon and Yucatan.

America and the Political Horror

An American Dream starts with a political bang—"I
met Jack Kennedy in November, 1946."—and abruptly
becomes Mailer's most nonpolitical book. It sig-
nals an end to a phase in Mailer's career, an obsession
with politics in many styles—from science, to philosophy, to art, before going (almost out of sight) to
magic. Throughout his evolving radicalism, he fixes on
one target—totalitarianism, an evil that makes him
view his period as "our most subtle and dear totalitarian time" (*ADV*, 18). To resist this "horror" Mailer
has let his fiction, journalism and private life mark
time to politics: "I have been running for President
these last ten years in the privacy of my mind, and it
occurs to me that I am less close now than when I
began" (17). As a political observer, Mailer also runs
on "privacy." His unique and marginal views take on
their greatest value once the current facts and theories
clear away. In his approach to the political scene, he
resembles a free-lance Eric Sevareid, eyeing the "horror" at the abyss.

How "totalitarianism" may evolve in America
shows up in *The Naked and the Dead*. The Fascist
Cummings says "If there's a war soon it'll help"
(426), and the novel dramatizes the belief that
World War II has been a try-out of American fascism
under way. Cummings calls "the concept of fascism"
a "dream" that started in the "wrong country," Ger-
many, and that "America is going to absorb that
dream, it's in the business of doing it now" (321).
Cummings—"the interpreter of twentieth-century

man" (313) — takes up a form of Hitlerism, and works on a midwestern leftist, Hearn, who is equally attracted and repelled by these dark prophecies. Grudgingly Hearn "absorbs" his lessons, bowing to his superior's sharp logic in assailing Marxist doctrine. After a briefing by Cummings, Hearn usually feels "shame and self-disgust and an impossible impotent anger" (326). Yet minutes earlier, he has admitted to the General, "We're moving toward greater organization, and I don't see how the left can win that battle in America" (320). On the final night of his life, Hearn reviews his history lesson and makes a stand: "Rely on the blunder factor. Sit back and wait for the Fascists to louse it up" (585). Such passivity accents why Hearn's "Time Machine" is subtitled "The Addled Womb" (328) — or how American liberalism has decayed before the postwar period. Or, in Cummings' language: "The root of all the liberals' ineffectiveness comes right spang out of the desperate suspension in which they have to hold their minds" (174). Cummings, on the other hand, acts on what he foresees: "The route to control could best masquerade under a conservative liberalism" (718). But Cummings is only a stand-in villain, for the real political villain is the American temperament which "sits back and waits" for warmongers to make its history.

The political stuff in *The Naked and the Dead* shows how Mailer relies on old ways of looking at things. Armies and their generals are after all pat symbols, pro or con, for authoritarian politics. The futility of following politics — in the style of political science — will catch up with Mailer, but not before he puts certain theories of the Left into action.

In 1948 he campaigned for Henry Wallace, the presidential candidate on the Progressive Party ticket. This support of Wallace, tagged by many as a Commie pawn, was Mailer's final gesture of American liberalism. In that campaign he blamed American capitalism for most postwar problems with Russia — an updated view of America through Cummings' eyes, believing the country was using Hitlerism to let loose the new American dream of world power. After the defeat of Wallace, Mailer cooled it with an American liberalism turning moderate and weak through alignment with political parties. But the national "horror" was expanding, and to counteract it Mailer realigned himself far to the Left of Wallace—as a radical leftist with an opportunistic grip on Marxist doctrine.

A low-keyed support of Marxism had already shaped *The Naked and the Dead*. The "Time Machines" zeroed in on average soldiers exploited before the war by a free-enterprise system that led to the Depression. These victims had become soldiers, spiritless and insecure, ready-made cannon fodder for the American warlords. Their bitterness toward society kept in step with apathy toward democratic ideals and other patriotic gimmicks for undertaking the war. Mailer's off-stage Marxist tone in his first novel worked itself out to the high-keyed "revolutionary socialism" in *Barbary Shore*.

There Mailer put forward this political slice of modern history. Once Marxism was pure; its revolutionary doctrine offered health, security and sanity to mankind. After Marx's death, the visionary Trotskyites gave up power to the reactionary, self-absorbing Stalinists of the Soviet Union. Revolutionary socialism as a political force ran dry. On the opposing side, capitalism, in its American form (Hitler's game according to Jeffersonian rules), had grown as reactionary as Russian communism. And the result, a worldwide trend away from equality and freedom and toward privilege and regimentation.

Such political views cling to Mailer's characters, especially McLeod, whose life reflects the recent history of Soviet socialism. His nineteen years' affiliation with communism reads like a political primer, illustrating how Trotskyite altruism had degenerated into the Stalinism of the Nazi-Soviet pact, the purges, assimilations, forced labor, and imprisoned minds. After dropping out as "Hangman of the Left Opposition," McLeod comes to America, works for the State Department before his leftist sympathies prompt him to desert his new job and to marry Guinevere and retire into a Brooklyn boardinghouse. McLeod introduces himself to Lovett: "One might call me a Marxist-at-liberty" (35). McLeod can no longer find any practical value in Marxian ideals, and when not lost in rosy theory, he feeds on the anti-Soviet: "The historical function of La Sovietica is to destroy the intellectual content of Marxism" (241). With a mind hair-triggered between fancy and fact, McLeod comes out, crippled by guilt tied to castoff ideals—as a skeptic with a golden past.

The failure of revolutionary socialism also shapes the Guinevere-McLeod relationship. As a political symbol, Guinevere stands for the American proletarian, ignorant of political doctrine—"I don't know anything about politics" (31). Her marriage to McLeod highlights the passing of intellectual Marxism, brainwashed by mating with mindless capitalism. At her core, Guinevere is irrational energy feeding on materialistic desires—a style that suggests to the other boarders a way of forgetting the "subtle" totalitarianism of the times. And so McLeod, Hollingsworth, Lovett and even Lannie all fall under her spell of greenback energy, which thins their dread of the encroaching tyranny.

Leroy Hollingsworth, Guinevere's traveling companion, stands for the reactionary Right, the cold war's version of General Cummings. Now fascism turns more familiar and congenial; it even masquerades as part of the national heritage—does not Hollingsworth's organization sound like the F.B.I.? But the exact nature of his mission and the identity of his political group never come out. What emerges, instead, is a figure, rigid, cold, a psuedo-intellectual, minus spirit, a robot on the move to "Barbary." The novel ends with two Americans—Hollingsworth (the Fascist) and Guinevere (the capitalist) pulling up stakes, and if their symbolic mating works out, the authoritarian takeover in America will be complete.

As a washed-out opponent of the Right, Lannie Madison is a Trotskyite, a vessel for all those high-flown sentiments and altruistic schemes once the heartbeat of the Russian revolution. Her political effectiveness ended by the war, Lannie enters the post-war era like someone from a concentration camp, her mind crippled, her feelings sterilized, her speeches vague. Lannie, too, casts a spell—a reminder to others of the glorious ideals of the recent past. Even Mikey Lovett, the dissociated radical, tries to find in her some survival of faith in the betterment of man. But sex with Lannie (in the style of love-thy-Trotsky) brings fear and pain, like Lovett's exposure to dread, and Hollingsworth's recourse to cruelty—ways to justify their rejection of the political lessons offered by the unselfish Lannie. Mailer also makes Lannie a prophet when she speaks of her vision—the new state as a gigantic concentration camp, complete with brainwashing, mass deaths, and all other authoritarian techniques aimed at snuffing out individualism and human emotion. And Lannie is partially heeded. Just before his surrender to Hollingsworth, McLeod confesses to her that "it was you and not him who wore me down" (295). Yesterday's guilt over the failed revolution becomes contagious and now Lannie can see a new "innocent" McLeod, who must "forgive" her.

Judging from McLeod's and Lannie's political careers, the predominant shift in the Left has been from the authentic and sane to the inauthentic and insane, and only Mikey Lovett learns the way to reverse this trend. Still young enough to regenerate the Left, he knows how his amnesia has enabled him in an odd way to cope with the guilt and frustration of the older revolutionaries. Though once involved with Marxists, he has forgotten both their victories and defeats; he feels no responsibility for Stalin and the authoritarian Left. His amnesia does not begin to end until nearly halfway through the novel, when he remembers his early quest for political "equality" during his pre-war membership in "a small organization dedicated to a worker's revolution," and he realizes how "the revolution [has] been betrayed" (126), and finds himself just as committed to Trotskyism as Lannie. Not she but someone like Lovett must preserve the Socialist culture in the coming age, though the immediate future offers little hope.

And Mailer's working in Willie Dinsmore adds another sign of the eclipse of American socialism, once so promising, in the 1930's. Postwar America feeds on a deadly "fulfillment." Materialism fills the American "belly," satisfying the national urge for social betterment, while keeping the American mind "hungry." To compensate, political power in postwar America adapts to this cultural disparity, and leadership switches to the Hollingsworth, whose mental "hunger" or stunted intellect makes them ripe for irrational totalitarianism. Their ready-made followers are the Guineveres, whose craze for satisfying their physical "hunger" or vulgar materialism makes them easy political victims. Hollingsworth's and Guinevere's move to "Barbary" is Mailer's metaphor of the final shift to authoritarianism in America and eventually throughout the world. But there is a snag. Hollingsworth must first "finish certain of his obligations" (205). When all these "missions" are accomplished, where will power reside? "Will you always tell me what to do?" —says Guinevere, and Hollingsworth replies—"Over and over I will tell you what to do" (206). In political terms: The centralized state will assimilate all material wealth in America as democratic capitalism lapses into American fascism.

Mailer elects McLeod (the super-intellect) to explain what may postpone this process. War will be "permanent," but future wars will be a series of Pyrrhic victories, with everyone (even winners) losers: "The war begins again with a new alignment of forces, and to the accompaniment of famine and civil war, the deterioration continues until we are faced with mankind in barbary" (282). The probability of "mankind in barbary" partly depends on a mysterious "little object." It intrigues everyone except its owner, McLeod. Both Hollingsworth and Guinevere view it as something material—a means to power and wealth and even to what the new woman terms "royalty" (205). But McLeod hints that the "little object" embodies the great intellectual and spiritual ideals once the stuff of revolutionary socialism (192). But Trotsky is dead and McLeod's death soon will follow. But first, McLeod must insure that the future generations of revolutionary socialists retain enough hope to spark their resistance to political "barbarism."

Emerging from the pessimism throughout *Barbary Shore* is a faint optimism tied to the fate of the "little object." It eludes the paws of the barbarians on the move. Hollingsworth's final complaint—"now nobody will ever have it" (308)—misses what Lovett receives from McLeod—"I bequeath in heritage the remnants of my socialist culture" (311). Do Hollingsworth's ignorance of its transfer and Lovett's suitability to receive it offer Mailer's readers much hope? There are Lannie's final words to Lovett: "Oh, you are my brother . . . for there is blood on your cheek, and so we are wed" (309). Even as she pledges this reconciliation, she is taken into custody and hands over her political mission to her brotherly comrade. But with Trotsky, McLeod and other supports gone, Lovett can only take on a leftover allegiance to revolutionary socialism. Against the drift toward the Right, Mikey Lovett may be some sort of bulwark, but he is an alienated loner whose faith runs one-way into the self.

After *Barbary Shore* Mailer—as an unaligned radical—calls himself a "libertarian socialist" which "is equivalent to accepting almost total intellectual alienation from America" (ADV, 202). In 1955, Mailer—a "Marxian anarchist"—summarizes how he has "changed" in seven years: "I suppose part of the change in my 'social ken' is that politics as politics interests me less today than politics as a part of everything else in life" (271).

In *The Deer Park* sex, not politics, takes center stage, but totalitarianism is at the root of every action. Mailer's style of political writing has gone underground, matching America's totalitarianism, grown so subtle that the didactic speeches and debates that cluttered *Barbary Shore* would sound like foreign history. Totalitarianism now stains every level of American life, including what Mailer spotlights in his third novel—the crisscrossed mores of politics and sex. At Desert D'Or, sexual license parades on the surface, but authoritarian politics operates underneath. In the Preface Mailer quotes Mouffle D'Angerville's account of Louis XV's "Deer Park"—"*Apart from the evil which this dreadful place did to the morals of the people, it is horrible to calculate the immense sums of money it cost the state.*" Mailer's Hollywood stands for an aristocracy of sex, a phoney free-for-all, isolated from the repressive style of sex imposed by the economic and political powers in America. The sexual toleration Hollywood enjoys is a kind of reward for keeping alive outmoded, patriotic and sentimental myths that help delude the American people into believing American fascism will be remodeled democracy. Desert D'Or (outside the bedroom) cranks out and sugar-coats the prehistory of American totalitarianism, which, when it is established, will allow the Cummings and the Hollingsworths to dictate sexual codes that will deaden everyone. Until then, dirty sex is tolerable so long as Hollywood uses its canned art to extoll Americanism.

At odds with Hollywood's rapport with the Center

is Charles Eitel, who may either keep his personal integrity or give in to the financial and social powers, the rubber stamp of an authoritarian government. For a time he rebels. While appearing before a Subversive Committee in Congress investigating his alleged leftist sympathies, he dares to admit once saying: "Patriotism is for pigs" (26). His skepticism exposed, Eitel plans to produce the original version of "Saints and Lovers"—an exposé of the romance between totalitarianism and sentimentality in the mass media. Eitel naturally irritates the reactionaries, especially Dorothea O'Faye, an ultrapatriotic gossip columnist whose "copy was filled with shadows of subversion in the movie industry" (18). Most of Eitel's former friends cover up their suspicion and resentment. Actually Eitel has played no political favorites, yet "guilt by association" (shadows of McCarthyism) has stamped him "pink," and he is ostracized both socially and professionally. But his rebellion soon ends, once he alienates Elena and prostitutes his movie script. Filled with self-pity, he fully realizes the defeat in accepting a dual amnesty—political pardon from Congressman Richard Crane, and social whitewash from Dorothea and the others. Eitel's public surrender, addressed to Crane's Committee, contains such phrases as "proud to be able to contribute my share to the defense of this country against all infiltration and subversion" (305). Eitel's defeat as artist and man serves as a coda to Mailer's belief that politics is "a part of everything else in life."

The next four years (1955–59) point up Mailer's accent on the personal and the intuitive in his approach to politics. As a "Marxian anarchist," he severs all ties with the American index to political identity. Orthodox socialism has become passé, and Mailer puts forth revolutionary remedies strange to Marxist dogma—"A new revolutionary vision of society" which must "explore" beyond "that jungle of political economy which Marx charted . . . and . . . engage the empty words, dead themes, and sentimental voids of that mass-media whose internal contradictions twist and quarter us between the lust of the economy . . . and the guilt of the economy which must chill us with authority" (ADV, 437). This shift from political textbook to national psyche also shows up in "Buddies, or the Hole in the Summit," Mailer's fragmentary comic play (412–21). Here Eisenhower and Khrushchev banter and haggle as private individuals running on mutual fear and respect. Naked, without their public images, each personality collides with his "only equal in the whole world." Personality—as the new stuff of American politics—also triggers Mailer's way-out wisdom for the democrats—draft Ernest Hemingway as presidential candidate in 1956, a winner with "energy," "charm," and "political sex appeal" (313).

The coming of Jack Kennedy (Hemingway's shadow in the White House) results in Mailer's final dialogue with the Center in *The Presidential Papers*, dedicated to President Kennedy. The persona Mailer adopts is that of "a court wit, an amateur advisor" (1), but he is still hellbent on making his opinions carry weight with the public. He begins by saying that the President has every qualification for greatness but one—imagination (3). Since "nothing is more exceptional than to introduce a new idea into America" (9), Mailer's strategy centers on fresh ways of looking at things—to become in effect the President's imagination, to change politics from a science of probability to "the art of the possible" (4). To counteract "featureless, symptomless diseases" (7) in the body politic, Mailer suggests making the natural use of human nature the basis of politics. The result is existential politics: "It has a basic argument; if there is a strong ineradicable strain in human nature, one must not try to suppress it or anomaly, cancer, and plague will follow. Instead one must find an art into which it can grow" (22). Mailer then applies this principle to current American politics.

"Superman Comes to the Supermarket" covers the 1960 Democratic Convention, one which "began as one mystery and ended as another" (28). At its "edge" stands John F. Kennedy—the future existential statesman—whose uniqueness makes him an enigma to his own political machinery and a transcendental force for the American people. Mailer pronounces Kennedy most fit to revitalize the national imagination. The reasons are obvious. What presidential candidate has ever possessed a personality so tuned to The American Dream—youth, energy, intelligence, sex appeal, wartime heroism, marriage to a beautiful woman, and even, membership in a Church formerly taboo to would-be presidents. Jack Kennedy even fits Mailer's political dream—a leader with enough psychic-drama left over for his people or an artist as President.

Mailer as "advisor," also sticks to the ways of the artist, especially with his need for a radical break with "political ritual and vocabulary" (152). "Classical politics begins with the notion that a great many facts and a few phenomena are hard, measurable, and concrete, and thus may be manipulated to produce corrective results. Existential politics . . . begins with the separate notion that we live out our lives wandering among mysteries, and can construct the few hypotheses by which we guide ourselves only by drawing into ourselves the instinctive logic our inner voice tells us is true to the relations *between* mysteries" (269).

Besides existential politics—"Totalitarianism has been the continuing preoccupation of this book" (175). And just as conventional party labels cannot express what is necessary and proper in politics, modern totalitarianism cannot be explained in the old doctrinaire way: "totalitarianism is better understood if it is regarded as a plague rather than examined as a style of ideology" (175). No faction can cope with the threat of the new totalitarianism. The reason why both the old Right and Left are powerless is that both have the "disease" of the Center. Opposition to the real enemy, the Center, must work through what Mailer terms the "new Left" and the "new Right" (78). In the Buckley Debate Mailer lists the symptoms of the disease of the Center. They include a cold sameness or a mad incongruity in architecture, tasteless food, denuded nature, motivational research, lifeless language—"a disease . . . so prevalent, insidious and indefinable that I choose to call it a plague" (165). Minus concentration camps and political parties, "totalitarianism has slipped into the body cells and psyche of each of us. It has been transported, modified, codified, and inserted into each of us by way of the popular arts, the social crafts, the political crafts, and the corporate techniques" (184). It has grown "peculiarly American," as "dear" to America as any other ideal of the national heritage.

But Mailer still has hope for curing the national disease. The "possible beginnings" of an end to totalitarianism show up in President Kennedy's style of personality, which makes him an artist of American manners—"(by the cavalier style of his personal life and the wistfulness of his appreciation for the arts) the possible beginnings of a Resistance to the American totalitarianism" (183). This "Resistance" will grow stronger only if future presidents "shift . . . the mind of the American politician to existential styles of political thought" (5).

Mailer's "unspoken" shock and grief immediately after Kennedy's death shapes *Cannibals and Christians*, a book in which existential politics gives up the ghost. The Dallas aftermath brings to the "arena" President Johnson and his Great Society whose advent marks the end of the "art of the possible" in American politics. "Jack Kennedy may not have been as skillful a politician as Lyndon Johnson, but he had one hundred times as much effect on the styles and modes of American life, on the desires of Americans, on what they finally demanded from life; so Jack Kennedy had a revolutionary effect on American life" (56). But

"Lyndon Johnson is a triumph of spirit, wholly scientific" (67). A one-time "appreciation for the arts" in the White House has fizzled into an age of pop art done up in Texan style. L. B. J.'s takeover has pushed America deeper into the "plague," and nearer the world of *Barbary Shore*.

The image—America on the march toward barbarism—unifies "In the Red Light: A History of the Republican Convention in 1964." Journalism sharpens to a fine art, as Mailer spotlights those nuances that give an otherwise so-so convention a psychic-drama all its own—Governor Romney who "looked like a handsome version of Boris Karloff"—or Governor Rockefeller whose "eyes . . . had the distant lunar glow of the small sad eyes you see in a caged chimpanzee or gorilla" (31, 32). To expose these half-blooded monsters and beasts Mailer relies on a strategy carried over from *An American Dream*—a concentration on mood, magic and manners that make for a larger view of American history out of joint. Behind his flip satire and black humor, he brings out a vision of the new men (computerized Hollingsworths) in the guise of new conservatism leading America back to deadly primitivism: "Civilization was worn thin in the center and to the Left the black man raised his primitive cry; now to the far Right were the maniacal blue eyes of the other primitive" (34). Echoing General Cummings' prophecy, the new Right—keyed to "red light" —resembles the fanaticism once on the loose in The Third Reich: "The mood of this convention spoke of a new kind of society. Chimeras of fascism hung like fogbank . . . The American mind had gone from Hawthorne and Emerson to the Frug, the Bounce, and Walking the Dog, from *The Flowering of New England* to the cerebrality of professional football in which a quarterback must have not only heart, courage, strength and grace but a mind like an I.B.M. computer. It marks the turn we have taken from the Renaissance" (28). This "turn" also takes in the new

Left and the stand-by Center: "The Establishment . . . had a new leader, a mighty Caesar had arisen, Lyndon Johnson was his name, all hail, Caesar" (43). Under the aegis of L. B. J., America becomes the twentieth century Rome, the giver of laws and Coca-Cola, whose roads lead to "Barbary" dressed up in American manners.

The spread of the American "plague" to the international scene leads Mailer to the "arena" of the conflict in Vietnam. As a kind of sardonic dove, he joins the current opposition to American policy. Any attempt "to justify our role in Vietnam on legal grounds is criminal" because we are "in violation of the Treaty of the Geneva Conference of 1954" (72). He also ridicules the State Department's "domino theory," and calls Vietnam "faceless," a culture outside American experience, which makes for the same "emotional participation . . . if we were to fight a war with the inhabitants of the planet of Mars" (73). Mailer then switches to his own thesis on the escalation of the war. It springs from "a secret motive" in President Johnson, "psychic in its nature . . . that the mystery of Vietnam revolves around the mystery of Lyndon Johnson's personality" (74). The key to the "mystery" lies in Johnson's "ego which [has] the voracity of a beast" (75) and which whets his dilemma —how to outshine the magnetism of Jack Kennedy, dubbed America's "leading man" or "the movie star come to life as President" (170). "Famished for popularity," President Johnson begins to feel that "The Great Society is a dud": "The President believed very much in image. He believed the history which made the headlines each day was more real to the people than the events themselves. It was not the Negro movement that possessed the real importance, it was the Movement's ability to get space in the papers" (70). And, "So the President needed another issue. Then it came to the President. Hot damn. Vietnam" (71).

Mailer further explores the "mystery" by calling Johnson "alienated" but not—"from power, he is the most powerful man in the United States, but he is alienated from judgment, he is close to an imbalance which at worst could tip the world from orbit" (76). Such alienation in a leader makes for greater anxiety in his nation: "The great fear that lies upon America is not that Lyndon Johnson is privately close to insanity so much as that he is the expression of the near insanity of most of us, and his need for action is America's need for action; not brave action, but action; any kind of action; any move to get the motors going. A future death of the spirit lies close and heavy upon American life, a cancerous emptiness at the center which calls for a circus" (77–78). Far from the main "arena" at home, the Vietnamese war turns into a barbaric sideshow—or as Mailer quips: "If World War II was like *Catch-22*, this war will be like *Naked Lunch*" (85). His approach to Vietnam is an outgrowth of his views on the cold war. As for the choice between capitalism and communism, "there is no man alive who can say at this point which system will perpetrate the greater harm upon mankind" (80). And so, "I say: end the cold war. Pull back our boundaries to what we can defend and to what wishes to be defended. Let Communism come to those countries it will come to. Let us not use up our substance trying to hold onto nations which are poor, underdeveloped, and bound to us only by the depths of their hatred for us" (80).

The cold war, Vietnam, L. B. J. or no matter what political topic shows up in *Cannibals and Christians*, the stuff of politics has left Mailer. His so-called political essays (lumped in the opening section entitled "Lambs") read more like mood sketches on national manners: "And as I left the arena, there was a fire engine and the cry of a siren and the police with a gaunt grim look for the end of the week. There had been a fire burning, some small fire" (45). Judging by his tone Mailer is leaving, not only the Republican Convention, but the whole "arena" of American politics. Hope for a Renaissance tied to existential politics has backtracked to despair in the face of current signs, especially a Vietnamese war zooming into high gear because "this country wishes to have an empire" (81). In such bleakness, Robert Kennedy offers a tenuous hope: "I have affection for Bobby Kennedy. I think something came into him with the death of his brother . . . Something compassionate, something witty, has come into the face. Something of sinew" (58). And John Lindsay (now mayor of New York) is "okay" and a "great guy" (64). Otherwise, the current style of democracy has turned America into a "rot of wet weeds" (52), and totalitarianism is so rooted in American life that any "Resistance" through politics would cover too small a part of the culture.

Yet the "political pieces done after the writing of An American Dream" (xi) update Mailer's vision of American politics—"a world of nightmare; psychopaths roved" (34). The cultural backdrop for Rojack's murder shows up in the "national mood," a cluster of political symptoms of the "plague" in a country—"fearful, half-mad, inauthentic"—who (like Rojack) "needed a purge" (34). Even Mailer's "explanation" for Vietnam centers on murder as the "national mood," in that "we are sinking into the swamps of a plague and the massacre of strange people seems to relieve the plague" (91). The political tone throughout Cannibals and Christians bears the mark of An American Dream, Mailer's first novel after ten years of "leading a life which was a trifle too pointless and a trifle too full of guilt and my gullet was close to nausea with the endless compromises of an empty liberal center" (26)—a mood that may be the beginning of the end of the political Mailer.

Such a stage is set in Cannibals and Christians. Existential politics (plus much exposition) gives way to politics as magic (minus any explanation). As in

An American Dream Mailer's style of magic is archly naive. It comes out in his recurring image of the assembly at the Goldwater Convention "as the children shaping up for the game" (10), "as a big football game" (26). Despite his disgust at politics turning all-American, Mailer keeps his eye on the action that transcends the playground—"it is the function of games to keep dreams, dread and surrealism out in the night where they belong" (14). But in all allusions to such magic, Mailer's mind stays uninvolved, his manner aloof, and politics becomes a "mystery" which Mailer no longer wants to solve.

A preview of Mailer's dampened craze for politics takes place in *An American Dream*. It begins like a political novel lifted from headlines, as a former "Congressman Stephen Richards Rojack, Democrat from New York" recalls his earlier meeting with Jack Kennedy which led to his marriage to Deborah Kelly, a strategy with a view that "the road to President might begin at the entrance to her Irish heart" (2). But once Rojack's dream begins, politics abruptly ends. In terms of the self, a public view gives way to a private vision. His exposure to murder linked to "magic, dread, and the perception of death" exhausts all possibilities for a life in politics. Marx's axiom— "quantity changes quality" (140)—takes effect once Rojack locks himself in a one-man dream at America's abyss. The quality of his acquaintance with the world of Jack Kennedy—a rapport with America's public romance of the politician-turned-statesman in the White House—turns remote in the presence of his "secret frightened romance with the phases of the moon" (7). But the quality of Rojack's experience is American in so far as Marx's axiom applies to the national scene. The American Dream of public life as an outlet for individual growth is dead, and all of America's frontiers (even Kennedy's belated "New Frontier") are closed to the individual on the move. The last frontier for personal growth passes outside

America, onto a map, psychic, private. Public life in the Sixties makes an individual faceless—a lesson known to the incestuous Barney Kelly whose remote control power hovers over every political action, including those Goldwater "children" playing at their "game" far from America's abyss. Under the present system of politics, an American must learn that it is better to be oneself than to be President. Rojack's dream, after a false political start, settles on the "mysteries" of murder and suicide, and Mailer's novel leaves the political "arena" quickly and permanently —as if a momentary mood (of the Goldwater Convention) had also taken hold of Mailer at work on Rojack's dream—"Politics was now open however to the disease of the bored-magic" (CC, 31).

Like *An American Dream, Cannibals and Christians* starts with political essays but ends with private visions. The way Mailer structures his "collection of writings from 1960" tells much about his future approach to politics: "Their order of appearance is, however, somewhat reversed . . . so the intellectual progression of the book is from the present forward to the past" (xi). In his "present" setup, political essays fall under the caption—"Lambs"—minor and expendable offerings alongside other more crucial concerns. As a result, the facts of politics give way to the feel of a culture headed toward a breakup. No longer is it possible to imagine "some optimistic love affair with the secret potentialities of this nation . . . The romance seems not even tragic or doomed, but dirty and misplaced" (71–72). America's burnt-out romance carries over into Mailer's new mood toward politics. Instead of "contend[ing] with the relations between miracles (for how else can politics appear at the top?) "politics (in a practical sense) involves the monotony of "statistics and programs and situation papers and debater's tricks . . . and worst of all saying the same thing day in, day out, week, week, month after month until your soul begins to die, because repetition, kids, kills the soul, and even as it is dying and the manner gets empty and the rhetoric more flat" (64). Mailer retaliates with *An American Dream*, in which manners get more full, and the rhetoric, more sharp, as a nonpolitical Rojack saves his body, and breaks even with his soul. In the first part of *Cannibals and Christians*, Mailer centers on the upside down manners of a Christian nation turned cannibalistic, and indirectly shows the political climate that never got into *An American Dream*. In the Sixties, America has grown top-heavy with totalitarianism, and Mailer (like Rojack) acts like a man who has glimpsed the "horror" at the top. The time seems ripe for Mailer's goodbye to politics, or (at least) for his compromise—a "secret frightened romance" with politics in time.

6

The Power Index
Rebellion from the Bottom

Mailer's vision of a rebellion by minorities whose basic strategy is psychopathy and violence begins in *The White Negro* (1957). It is rooted in Mailer's obsession with power, which makes him that kind of writer whose ambition "is to become consecutively more disruptive, more dangerous, and more powerful" (ADV, 22).

A wartime army is structured power—a fact that Mailer reluctantly takes to in *The Naked and the Dead*. Sanctioned by a patriotic clamor for victory through piety, this power hierarchy rattles fear through the ranks. On the lower echelons the power-figure is the mindless and instinctual Sergeant Croft. From his childhood Sam Croft has pushed to control other men, and he enters the army as a ready-made Sergeant—"Leading the men was a responsibility he craved: he felt powerful and certain at such moments" (28). But once he reappraises death in war and rids himself of the fear of dying, he settles on a mystic quest for absolute power. With his influence over men cut short by his inferior mind, Croft senses that he can take on added power only if he becomes number one at subduing nature. His quest shows itself most consciously during his attempt to climb Mount Anaka, which proves too high a challenge. Near the end, he experiences just enough doubt to justify his feeling "rested by the unadmitted knowledge that he had found a limit to his hunger" (701). Croft can never make it as a younger Cummings.

At the top of the hierarchy the power quest works on a more conscious and rational level. General Cummings is the prophetic spokesman for power morality.

> For the past century the entire historical process has been working toward greater and greater consolidation of power . . . Your men of power in America, I can tell you, are becoming conscious of their real aims for the first time in our history. (321–22)

As a part of this historical trend, only Cummings knows how unstable his power-role is. His leadership —its power based on the wartime military with "every man in it fitted into a fear ladder" (176)—resists as much as aids his urge "to make youself an instrument of your policy" (82)—a feat that must be accomplished before the war ends, when the concentrated military power will fade (177). The General has a knack for power, enough to reach his goal; his superior mind gains essential lessons from military logistics, politics, economics and history. But Cummings has other characteristics which hinder his quest for higher power, especially his latent homosexuality, which sparks his intense talks with Hearn, and which stamps the entries in his private journal. Paralleling Croft's failure with Mount Anaka are Cummings' own "final sustaining ironies." With "sloughed off Hearn" in his past, with the absurd conclusion to his Anopopei campaign in his future, the General at least can muster this much comfort: "In the final analysis there was only necessity and one's own reactions to it" (402).

The invitation to power continually attracts Lieutenant Hearn. A foil to Cummings and Croft in their respective power quests, he is a kind of middleman—commanded before he commands. In either role, Hearn shows an ambiguous attitude toward power—fascinated with its theory while resisting its practice, which disappoints Cummings who once saw Hearn as a potential equal. Finally Hearn is given command of the I and R squad, his opportunity to act on his belief in liberal and humanitarian leadership. But when challenged by the totalitarian and psychopathic Croft, Hearn falters and feels "disgusted with himself" (532). This "disgust" grows every time he uses power. Hearn's hatred of the authoritarian style of power morality hinges on his unconscious identification with what Cummings had called "the archtype of twentieth century man" whose "natural role . . . was anxiety." In fact, there are times when Cummings' power ideology almost merges with Hearn's. " 'Man had to destroy God in order to achieve Him, equal Him.' Cummings again. Or had Cummings said it? There were times when the demarcation between their minds was blurred for him" (392).

Is there any analogy with Mailer as author? Hearn's failure to see the "demarcation" between his and Cummings' beliefs hints at a similar uncertainty in Mailer, but Mailer's approach to the operations of power is clear-cut. Power mushrooms during war and sometimes takes over part of the American Establishment. Military power is so institutionalized that its action is always down and never up the hierarchy of command. Those with power correspond to the civilian elite. Those on the "fear ladder," soldier or civilian, must conform. Mailer's early views on power accent the postwar scene and not the ideals of his later strategy for power consolidation in the style of the rebels, not the regulators.

In *Barbary Shore*, the spotlight shifts from power as the object of a quest, making the concept of power more abstract and vague. But the power drive still lingers in both characterization and action. World colossi replace generals and lieutenants. The political Left and Right vie for supremacy. Their respective figures, McLeod and Hollingsworth, engage in a power struggle in which ideologies clash minus the show of personalities. Of the two, the leftist McLeod stands for yesterday's power, giving way to Hollingsworth's type, more tuned to the technological age.

The younger Hollingsworth is a power enthusiast who regards his victim with a hatred mixed with awe toward "a gentleman like yourself who commanded so many men" (235). As a throwback to Mailer's earlier power moralist, Hollingsworth looks like an ugly kind without a father. This inheritor of Cummings' power metaphysics has a low-keyed mind, and lacks the grace and style of the social elite. But the power organization that Hollingsworth inherits looks like a latter-day army machine. As in *The Naked and the Dead*, supreme power takes to totalitarianism, the political Right, and the American Establishment, while the authority of the political Left passes away—its long shot chance for power put on Lovett's vigilant exile.

The style of power in *The Deer Park* shifts from the political to the social. The vast power organizations which filled *Barbary Shore* fade out, except for a stand by Congressional Investigating Committee. What Mailer emphasizes, instead, is power based on economic means and social prestige. Military and political hierarchies pass the reins to the social group. Not institutions but personalities take over, as impersonal and systematic control gives way to intimate and complicated influence.

Of all the characters, Marion Faye pinpoints the link between *The Deer Park* and *The White Negro*. As the prototype of the White Negro, Faye combines a passion for power and a flair for violence with a psychopathic disposition. Power, even when rooted in evil, is ever the highest good. Once everyone at Desert D'Or plays the game of hypocrisy inherent in the social code, Faye adopts his own style of power morality—a private and relative code based on an awareness that moral minds rationalize immoral actions. He finds that his best tactic for maintaining sway over others results from training himself to be a perfect psychopath. Whatever stirs up emotion and guilt in others must be turned into apathy and composure for him. Soon he ends up deadened by all sexual taboos.

To master added power through greater self-control forces him to experiment with more crucial taboos, such as murder; he realizes how such justifiable violence can pyramid him to unlimited authority, if the violent act is committed by an individual free from institutionalized guilt.

Although Faye fails to show up in *The White Negro*, Mailer's essay still retains Faye's dramatic approach to the power quest. Here Mailer centers on the marginal man, especially the Negro, the psychopathic personality, the hipster, and a psychic revolution aimed at affirming the nihilistic one against the totalitarian many, but in the background power is still the motivating force. But Mailer's framework of power morality has shifted. From its earlier phrasing in terms of military and political forces, power has become a personal goal of individuals. This makes the quest for power positive, in that it accents individual growth instead of group welfare, which is the stuff of the oppressive power of the cultural establishment. Without the crutch of any "ism," the hipster turns into a non-political radical, but he does not pass into an ideological vacuum: "It is not that the hipster is reactionary, it is rather that in a time of crisis, he would look for power, and in the absence of a radical spirit in the American air, the choices of power which will present themselves are more likely to come from the Right than the moribund liberalities of the Left" (*ADV*, 374). Mailer's gesture toward the Right as the lesser evil during "the absence of a radical spirit" may seem startling, since in the public mind he stands solid with the Left. But faced with the following national power structure, a radical must prepare to any direction (even a cutthroat alliance with the Right) to survive.

Opposed to amoral authority (only power for the sake of power), Mailer's ideal kind of power would be courageous, and as honest as rebellion against the authoritarians may allow. To cut out amorality, persons with power must have keen sensitivity. To the question—"Whom do you hate?"—Mailer replies: "People who have power and no compassion, that is, no simple human understanding" (271). Where are the insightful and compassionate people to be found? Looking over the various classes, Mailer believes that the social minorities, particularly Negroes, make up the greatest ratio of sensitive people—the future source for power moralists.

With not one Negro (white or black) worked in his fiction or essays, Mailer plunges into *The White Negro*, which is about much more than Negroes. Although he runs second to more crucial concerns, the Negro does appeal to Mailer for one key trait. Racial prejudice preps the American Negro to be more aware and sensitive—two unusual social virtues that mark him as "the source of Hip" (340). Awareness takes to the black man every time he encounters the white man's indifference or bigotry—"The Negro has the simplest of alternatives: live a life of constant humility or everthreatening danger" (341). After enough tense social scenes, the more sharp and calloused Negro can instantly sift out friends and enemies from among the countless so-so Whites. For the Negro, awareness equals social survival. Sensitivity—a kind of mutual empathy expressed by individuals regardless of race—is what the Negro seeks but seldom finds, which leads to his pinpointing "soul" or feeling as the key to a superior person, among themselves and the Whites.

But Mailer is not parceling out Hipness to all American Negroes. The Negro may be "the source of Hip" but not all Negroes are hipsters. But since the squares (those unaware and insensitive) far outnumber the hipsters in either race, Mailer favors the Negro because he makes up the majority of hipsters (a minority of a minority) in America where the majority of Negroes stay "square." For this reason Mailer does not push for black supremacy, nor even pro-Negro liberalism. To claim that Mailer stereotypes the

Negro as a dancing master, nighttime pleasure-boy, or sex expert misses the fact that Mailer puts across no social analysis of the American Negro. Instead he limits himself to projecting a few Negroes (the hipsters) as an elite minority within a minority, all set to overturn the WASP at the top. But the accelerated change in American power and Negro status following *The White Negro* has upset Mailer's timetable for the hip Negro on the move. Mailer knows that the new breed of hip Negroes see their rise as a social force and America's growth as a world power as a one-way strategy. Non-White members at the U.N. immediately react to racial strife in Birmingham or New York. To keep up with America straddled between world leadership and Negro militancy, Mailer has up dated his power index to fit the new hipster who has bypassed the color line.

In *An American Dream*, the expected power-figure as White Negro does not appear. Instead, Rojack (all-White and a square by Shago Martin's standards) enters a world that Mailer once earmarked for the Negro.

> The Negro, secretly fixed upon magic — that elixir of nature which seems to mediate between God and Devil — has never made his peace with Christianity, or mankind. The Negro in the most protected recesses of his soul still does not know if he is a part of mankind, or a special embodiment of nature suspended between society and the gods. (*PP*, 190)

This is the stuff of Rojack's dream-existence. But Negro values never shape his dream. Instead of a Negro revolutionary, what does materialize in Mailer's fourth novel is a concept of power, revised almost out of sight.

Power, in Rojack's dream, passes for a nightmare because it no longer relates to the individual. As the world's leader, America has turned into a vast power-machine no human can control, not even the few at the top.

Stationed at the Waldorf Towers is Barney Oswald Kelly, the power-figure in the novel. As the Horatio Alger of the Nuclear Age, Kelly has risen from a Minnesota family as "poor as rats" (238) to where he has "made a million two hundred times" (3). Now his sphere of influence takes in world finance and politics, the Mafia, C.I.A. and mass media. But over and above Kelly, there is the magic of astrological power. In explaining how his millions pyramided through his superstitious play of the stock market, Kelly as a power theorist goes back to the root meaning of "influence," to some occult force flowing from the stars that works on human destiny. Finally, from the heights of American power, he realizes: " 'I decided the only explanation is that God and the Devil are very attentive to the people at the summit . . . There's nothing but magic at the top' " (246). Power morality has turned superhuman. The power moralist is nothing but a pawn in the universal struggle between good and evil. For Kelly, the self-made man is a myth, as is the American ideal of taking on power as a means of self-expression. Since his ego is not the moving force, the exercise of power results in boredom "infinite in its dimensions" (247). To compensate, he seeks "diversion" in a private exercise of power, by exploiting taboos such as anality, orgy and especially incest which "is the gate to the worst sort of forces" (246). Incest may lead to exposure at the hands of "One or the Other," but it is one of the few ways left to test and express the self. As an older Marion Faye who has made good, Kelly picks up a lesson known only to the pro at the top—that the psychopathic style with taboos is not the way to power, but is a way to keep the self in shape while the power accrues through the magic overhead. The Waldorf Towers may outclass the "Deer, Park," but Mailer's latest power figure (once "one of the hundred most important fellows around") acts disenchanted: "Today, *everybody* is important" (248). In the Sixties, American power has outgrown the individual. There is room at the top only for those willing to lose themselves in a world-wide release of energy which is as human as a computer.

Mailer's own discontent with the power quest shows up in Rojack—his first protagonist who turns his back on the power craze. Before his dream, Rojack's life reads like a success story, aimed toward a happy ending among the powerful. But murder forces him to review success in terms of the self. Though established power (police, society) threaten his survival, he still remains fascinated with its source, and it is no accident that Mailer retards Rojack's encounter with Kelly to the end. In his discussion of Robert Kennedy, Mailer echoes what Rojack discovers about the current style of American power: "A forceful political structure with a great number of particular heroes is a way to describe the Renaissance; a powerful political structure governed by faceless men is a way to describe the Mafia" (CC, 58). Just as Kennedy possesses "finally a face" for Mailer, so does Kelly for Rojack. But unlike Kennedy's, Kelly's face lies outside American experience—marked by incest, orgy and other private actions which no longer "matter" in a land where "public show" becomes the crucial index to practical power. Rojack begins to see how America has made Kelly into a corrupt version of the Renaissance man. Kelly's library—his "favorite" room—resembles a "royal chapel" fashioned in "late sixteenth century" with a "Venetian throne," a room "like the interior of a cave" (233, 234). In a room surfaced with history, Rojack hears Kelly's story, but the face mirrors no sense of history. It reflects, instead, an "interior" life, a rapport with taboos or an exercise of control over the self to offset the power over others. With his true nature (like his roomlike "cave") staying underground, Kelly—as a power-figure hooked to American history—must lose himself in a "public show," which makes him as "faceless" as the others.

As Kelly's guardian spook, Besse ("the most evil woman ever to live on the Riviera" [216]) comes out petty and spiteful; she constantly mouths platitudes sugared with "darlings," and shows bad manners toward the "old wop," Eddie Ganuci. This Mafia boss ends up as a comic figure who got lost in history. "Your daughter had the class of the angels" (220) — he tells Kelly, like an old Italian gangster turned into an unconscious buffoon of the Computer Age. Behind his Mafia "face," Uncle Eddie is a superstitious, fear-ridden, death-obsessed old man whose self-pity underlies his inability to understand and control his power-role. Of this trio at the top, only Kelly impresses Rojack, but not enough to convert him to the style of power that runs America.

Murder has made Rojack a misfit at the Waldorf Towers. As an intelligent man on a quest to perfect his manners and courage, he sees in Kelly and his clan the mannerisms of the mindless and spineless. To ride out his exposure to the "One or the Other," he must seek power, not over others, but over himself. Unlike Faye, Rojack prefers the psychic bottom to the social bottom, and the Waldorf, not Harlem, becomes his final testing ground. Once he discovers that survival at the top demands that the self be sacrificed to the power complex, and that incest and murder are twin "gates" to the top, he fears that he may end as another Kelly. To counteract this "promise of power" (254), Rojack "strolls," unaided, around a parapet, an individual daring to be at odds with the structures and men thirty stories high. Incest may be Kelly's gate, but murder makes for Rojack's exit. His need for total power over himself drives him to a foreign jungle far from the image of himself as a Kelly whose price for staying in America includes a dream that the index to power will again be a magic that is self-made.

Through Rojack, Mailer projects his own disenchantment with the power quest: "I don't know if I want power any more. I think I would rather be clear in my mind. The compromises one has to make in acquiring power dull the brain irreparably" (*CC*, 255). One "clear" reason for Mailer's fall out with power is the fast eclipse of the White Negro—a result of the accelerated change in Negro values and objectives, especially after the Washington demonstration for Negro rights in August of 1963.

Mailer—in his approach to the March on Washington—hints that the Negro Movement has passed over his style of revolution. He calls the total nonviolence "revolutionary genius," because violence during the march may have "alienated" millions of neutral whites: this revolution, at least, must observe a kind of golden mean—"A revolution withers if it is afraid of creating outrage, but it is killed in ambush if it accepts and attacks each and every possibility for outrage presented to it" (*Esquire*, Dec. 1963). This latter extreme points up the most recent shift in the Negro Revolution—a widespread recourse to violence and hatred, disunity in leadership, and the rise of Stokley Carmichael and "Get Whitey." Since 1964, violence (not discipline) has moved this revolutionary force. On the eve of "Black Power" and "White Backlash," Shago Martin (Mailer's first Negro character) enters *An American Dream* with a slice of Negro history.

Shago's appearance is brief (about twenty pages) but significant enough to make his presence felt throughout the latter half of the book. He is that updated Negro on the move in America. But Shago's future already lies in his past. He tells Rojack how he " 'did the Freedom Rider bit . . . I'm just the future, in love with myself, that's the future. I got twenty faces, I talk the tongues, I'm a devil, what's the devil doing on a Freedom Ride? Listen,' he said, building up force as he went, 'I'm cut off from my own lines, I try to speak from my heart and it gets *snatched*. That's Freedom Ride' " (188–89). So-called Freedom Rides may seem like pilgrimages to a future Utopia, but for today's Negro, they are expeditions into the

loss of identity and dignity. Nonviolence "rides" into
violence; soulfulness into callousness. This results in
the Negro experiencing the worst of two possible
worlds. The White world (the one to be emulated)
offers him its worst, while he sacrifices the best of his
Black world. Shago Martin, trapped in the flux of
1964, is the epitome of the Negro alienated from
racial history. In a milieu whose historical roots
equate black with evil, white with good, Shago passes
for a "lily-white devil," a satanic seducer of the white
world. "An elegant Negro with a skin dark as mid-
night" (179), he turns a classic white stereotype of
the Negro—as the darky (yeah-boss) entertainer—
into a ploy for getting money, kicks, status and fame.
His past career as a singer reads like a one-man assault
on white gullibility. The Negro as Trickster has in-
vaded mass media with a vengeance. On record al-
bums, his standard photograph advertises "a handsome face, thin and arrogant, a mask" (180). But
behind the "mask," Shago runs on a dream of the
Negro Revolution before the March on Washington
—the black man's Horatio Alger who has sung his way
from the Harlem Ghetto to "the Copa and Latin
Quarter," whose songs have always been pitched to
White Power. Before Rojack's dream begins, Shago's
style of "going smooth" highlights the social tactics of
Negroes, hellbent on success through assimilation into
the world of the WASP.

But *An American Dream* accents private, not social
reality, and Mailer (through Rojack's eyes) looks at
Shago Martin as a man acting on his own anxiety
dream. In his "enormous present," he is depicted as
one imprisoned in a colorless, rootless existence.
Negro and underworld values (switchblades, mari-
juana, a "harsh" song beat) stick despite his rise to
"the big divide" between Lenox Avenue and the Waldorf Towers. In the process he has kept losing his
blackness while emulating whiteness until he realizes,
"I'm a sick devil, no doubt of that" (186). The

White Establishment—in a dream turned nightmare
—has turned into a sick god who speaks its toneless
ritual through mass media. Like Rojack, Shago has
also "wished to steal the secrets of the gods": " 'Cause
I can do the tongues . . . cause I let each accent pick
its note, every tongue on a private note, when I sing
it's a congregation of tongues, that's the spook in my
music, that's why they got to buy me big or not at all,
I'm not intimate, I'm Elizabethan, a chorus, dig?' "
(190). The versatility of the Renaissance Man has no
place in an age of mass communication. Shago has
assumed so many roles, has spoken so many tongues
that he now feels alienated from all racial and national history. The Negro as Trickster finally tricks
himself. In his present dilemma (in a colorless world
where militant Negroes condemn his Uncle Tom marriage to a white woman) he experiences a "dread"
similar to Rojack's. Shago, too, represents "a mind
racing between separate madnesses" (183). And so
Shago's present "dream" prefigures what Mailer elsewhere says: "more and more of the kids in Harlem
want not justice but revenge and threaten to become
implacable and grow not on liberty but power and so
must demand more and more before they have yet
anything at all" (CC, 62). But in Shago's case his last
crucial "demand" settles on self-knowledge. No longer
in search of power (either Black or White), he follows Rojack's quest for self-control, but in the style of
a black man—he must never "throw away (his) cool."
His chief tactic for perfecting control is to project the
dual manners of a Harlem hoodlum and a soulful
sophisticate—a code of manners unknown to Rojack,
who listens to Cherry explain that Shago would not
have used his switchblade in a "real fight," and that
"there's something clean about Shago" (196). Not
even murder blackens Rojack enough to make him
aware of Shago's "dream." "You're just an old dy-
namo out on the moon" (190)—Cherry tells Shago,
but Rojack never tells the reader the exact nature of
the Negro's "fear" and "dread." The narrator, instead,

plays the part of the good listener, and the scene reads like a Shago Martin monologue, which incidentally allows Mailer to show off his sharp ear for hip Negro dialect. Only Shago enters Rojack's dream, and exits with his own dream undisclosed and unresolved, except for an off-stage death which makes the stuff of *An American Dream* much more white than black.

In *Cannibals and Christians*, Mailer has also pushed the Negro problem off-stage. His near silence hints at his split with the Negro cause and its leaders, even though the major blame still lies with the American Establishment. Such inauthentic gestures, like the Civil Rights Act, have stressed the "protection of property rights" and not ("what the Negro was entitled to") "spiritual rights" (47). Meanwhile, the tempo of racial violence has "accelerated," and with it, one of Mailer's key theories on the strategy of revolution—violence in the style of the psychopath—was tested at the wrong time, in the wrong way.

At the heart of Mailer's theory on violence is his concept of the psychopath, which differs from the standard psychopath that shows up in textbooks. In the clinical sense, the psychopath or sociopath acts out his conflicts with social norms. His anti-social behavior stems from an emotional immaturity which urges him to gratify all his immediate desires. But what really singles him out is his incapacity to feel ordinary guilt after committing anti-social acts—a trait that marks him as a cold animal on the prowl to use others. Only rarely does the psychopath suspend his egoism. If confronted by the most stringent social taboos (cannibalism, incest, matricide) or the lesser taboo of appearing nude in public, the psychopath may experience some degree of social embarrassment and personal guilt, but not enough to keep him from reverting to apathy. Seeking gratification in all moments, indifferent to second thoughts and the long view, the psychopath is society's most aggressive outlaw, alienated from all things but himself.

In *The White Negro* Mailer both accepts and rejects the clinical view of the psychopath. Standard psychoanalysts, especially Robert Lindner, he quotes and affirms. But Mailer turns nonprofessional and impressionistic when he describes the style of the psychopath. The field of immediate gratification becomes the "enormous present"; or, to put forth psychopath energy means either to "swing," becoming "Hip," or to become "beat," turning "Square." After advising his readers to "encourage the psychopath in oneself" —Mailer says:

> It may be fruitful to consider the hipster a *philosophical psychopath*, a man interested not only in the dangerous imperatives of his psychopathy but in codifying, at least for himself, the suppositions on which his inner universe is constructed. By this premise the hipster is a psychopath, and yet not a psychopath but the negation of the psychopath, for he possesses the *narcissistic detachment* of the philosopher, that absorption in the recessive nuances of one's own motive which is so alien to the unreasoning drive of the psychopath. In this country . . . there has been room already for the development of the *antithetical psychopath* who extrapolates from his own condition, from the inner certainty that his rebellion is just, a radical vision of the universe which thus separates him from the general ignorance, reactionary prejudice, and self-doubt of the more conventional psychopath. (ADV, 343)

Mailer tries to impart a cause to Robert Lindner's "rebel without a cause." To be Mailer's kind of psychopath makes for an immediate transvaluation of values. Since man has turned too civilized, bogged down in a computer age which grinds out bigger and better minds while it stamps out human emotions, human minds continue to outgrow nervous systems, and Mailer's "antithetical" psychopaths backtrack to the primitive by "trying to create a new nervous system for themselves" (345). Moral values also take a new direction. The "more conventional psychopath" is totally amoral, more indifferent than opposed to society. Conventions simply do not exist. The "anti-thetical psychopath" may not be bound by conventions but he is at least bound by something—"a certain instinctive wisdom" (345). His "narcissistic detachment" makes him aware of society's threat to snuff out the individual—a threat which causes him to justify his external amorality. Lindner's psychopath may not have the power "to internalize the norm" but Mailer's psychopath can and does. Understanding the absurdity inherent in a social norm works the "anti-thetical psychopath" into a warlike opposition to the Cultural Establishment. But a revolutionary must also be an ideologist, and what links the "antithetical" to the "philosophical" is Mailer's belief that this new psychopath "extrapolates" from his antisocial experience "a radical vision of the universe." Already Mailer is tacking on a future to the psychopath's "enormous present." Immediate antisocial acts will transcend a one-man gratification, because the "philosophical psychopath" will sense how his actions contain revolutionary seeds for a culture without any worth-while cause.

In the past Mailer has singled out the Negro as a ready-made psychopath: "Hated from outside and therefore hating himself, the Negro was forced into the position of exploring all those moral wildernesses of civilized life which the Square automatically condemns as delinquent or evil or immature or morbid or self-destructive or corrupt" (348). Mailer's past strategy (even though the New Negro may be an early drop-out) puts the psychopath on the move for personal and social power. For the psychopath simply to have his kicks at the social bottom is not enough. He must also thoroughly get to know all the nuances in the social underworld—only possible through "codifying" his action when he takes over social taboos. As the conformists permit a sentimental "hang-up" on parent, church, and state or law to cut down their latent urge for power, the "philosophical" psychopath, instead, will allow his "narcissistic detachment" to free him of all inhibitions while engaging in a tabooed act—"The psychopath murders—if he has the courage—out of the necessity to purge his violence, for if he cannot empty his hatred then he cannot love, his being is frozen with implacable self-hatred for his cowardice" (347). It is the "philosophical psychopath's" capacity to seek power as a kind of metaphysical criminal which works in a topic that has concerned Mailer far beyond *The White Negro*.

That topic is violence, and Mailer would almost agree with Orwell. "If you want a picture of the future, imagine a boot stamping on a human face—forever" (*1984*). The mass of violence in *The Naked and the Dead* fits the facts of war. But fourteen years later, when asked how his attitude toward violence has changed, Mailer replies: "The ideal I had about violence changed 180 degrees over those years. Beneath the ideology in *The Naked and the Dead* was an obsession with violence. The characters for whom I had the most secret admiration, like Croft, were violent people. Ideologically, intellectually, I did disapprove of violence, though I didn't at the time of 'The White Negro'" (*PP*, 136). What Mailer later terms "inhuman" describes the violence depicted in *Barbary Shore*. One reason why civilization is passing into barbarism shows up in Lannie Madison's hallucinations of the mass extinction of human life in the concentration camps—a kind of violence that Mailer will later condemn as "large scale and abstract."

Mailer's new accent on violence occurred after *Barbary Shore*, though that novel itself foreshadowed a new artistic vision, one gradually "leading toward the violent and the orgiastic" (*ADV*, 106). *The Deer Park* continued this trend, stressing the "orgiastic" through Hollywood sex, the "violent" through psychopath Marion Faye. But Mailer waited until *The White Negro* before displaying his later theories of violence. Yet there, and elsewhere in *Advertisements*, he hedged on exactly how far he went in thinking violence justifiable. His tone wavered from a so-so assent to open support.

In *The Presidential Papers* Mailer takes up his theory of justifiable violence. Juvenile delinquency stems from "the national disease—it is boredom" (21). To avoid repression and anonymity, the juvenile delinquent must act on his inalienable right and existential duty to determine his own growth through welcoming "a need for danger" (15). Mailer offers other remedies: "the best way to combat juvenile delinquency was to give artistic outlet to the violence, creativity, and sense of pageantry which drives the average wild adolescent into disaster. Why not have medieval jousting tournaments in Central Park" (22). Mailer continually refers to boredom as a chief symptom of the national cancer that has paralyzed the individual in America—an offshoot of totalitarianism, which is "an insidious, insipid sickness demanding a violent far-reaching purgative" (134). One such "purgative" is violence. But every act of justifiable violence must follow a set style, the reverse of violence that is "large scale and abstract." Violence, to be justified, must grow out of a violent act limited to a particular instance and marked by personal intimacy.

Since a writer's acts at times express his thought, Mailer's stabbing of his second wife Adele in 1960 hinted at those nuances which make a violent act either justifiable or unjustifiable. According to Adele there was no reason why her husband knifed her. "He just came at me with a funny look in his eye." When arrested and urged to undergo psychiatric observation, Mailer replied: "It is very important to me not to be sent to some mental institution. I'm a sane man. If this happens, for the rest of my life my work will be considered as the work of a man with a disordered mind. My pride is that as a sane man I can explore areas of experience that other men are afraid of. I am sane" (*Time*, Dec. 5, 1960). Adjudged sane, Mailer was freed with his "pride" intact.

Just days before the knifing incident, in an inter-

view later printed in *Mademoiselle* (Feb. 1961),
Mailer introduced his concept of authentic violence,
in connection with Orwell's image of the heel in the
face of the dying man.

MAILER   If you're going to grind your heel into the face
    of a dying man, I still insist on the authority of my
    existential logic: let the act finally be authentic. If
    you're going to do it, *do it*.
INTERVIEWER   You mean enjoy it?
MAILER   The poor soul is going out of existence. You
    might as well enjoy yourself! If you're going to grind
    your boot in his face don't do it with the feeling,
    "I'm horrible, I'm psychotic, I should be in a bug-
    house." Do it.

Mailer sets up two opposing styles of violence—an
act that is inauthentic, unreliable and baseless and an
act that is authentic, trustworthy and authoritative.
As a follow-up to Mailer's "existential logic," "authentic" also stresses how this violent act agrees with ac-
tuality or fact. The inauthentic style of violence (like
the TV cult of the vicarious viewer) sanctioned by the
WASP Establishment passes over the fact that violence keeps increasing in America. To reintroduce the
fact, Mailer applies his theory of authentic violence to
his existential legislation concerning capital punishment. If not abolished, the state execution, at least,
should be converted into a "personal and a public
spectacle," where criminal and executioner are equally
matched in size, weapon, with the death certified by
Marquis Queensberry's rules. Then,

> The benefit of this law is that it might return us to
> moral responsibility. The killer would carry the other
> man's death in his psyche. The audience, in turn,
> would experience a sense of tragedy, since the execu-
> tioners, highly trained for this, would almost always
> win. In the flabby American spirit there is a buried
> sadist who finds the bullfight contemptible—what he
> really desires are gladiators. Since nothing is worse for a
> country than repressed sadism, this method of execu-

tion would offer ventilation for the more cancerous emotions of the American public. (*PP*, 11)

But authentic violence is even more useful to those engaged in the violent act. In the *Mademoiselle* interview Mailer puts forward the key to authentic violence.

> Let's use our imaginations. It means that one human being has determined to extinguish the life of another human being. It means that two people are engaging in a dialogue with eternity. Now if the brute does it and at the last moment likes the man he is extinguishing then perhaps the victim did not die in vain. If there is an eternity with souls in that eternity, if one is able to be born again, the victim may get his reward. At least it seems possible that the quality of one being passes into the other, and this altogether hate-filled human, grinding his boot into the face of someone, destroying the most private part of a person (remember, in the twentieth century one's sexual privates are no longer so private as one's face), in the act of killing, in this terribly private moment, the brute feels a moment of tenderness for the first time perhaps in all of his existence. What has happened is that the killer is becoming a little more possible, a little bit more ready to love someone.

To join the psychic elite in overcoming taboos, Mailer's psychopath must have courage gained by making his antisocial behavior as authentic as possible. Insensitive toward everything except his need for internal growth and external power, he must seek "moral responsibility" in violent actions once thought to be harmful to moral growth. Morality turns authentic once the absolute passes into the relative, with each individual acting on his own dos-and-don'ts. If the psychopath ever perverts his will to power, becoming susceptible to standard morality during violence, he instantly turns dishonest toward his victim and himself; and struck down by social and personal guilt, he will be adjudged insane and "psycho" by a triumphant society. But the authentic psychopath will keep his sanity intact by always using his "new nervous system" during the violent act. This new form of control enables him to concentrate his will on his action and his victim because authentic violence is conscious violence. Completely to realize one's self or to become absolutely self-aware at such moments takes in one limitation—the authentic psychopath must expose his will to his victim's reactions. Then he will remain authentic during violence, imparting his awareness to his victim and permitting his victim's recognition to impregnate his own psyche—the only way to invest the violence with moral energy. And for a moment, an immoral act (shaped by society) passed into an amoral deed (shaped by the psychopath) before the actual violence joins victim and victimizer into a moral relationship apart from all other moral systems.

For this "moral responsibility" to come over the "philosophical psychopath," he must experience a peculiar epiphany or a sudden manifestation of intimacy leading to love. Such an offbeat quest for love points up another cultural fact—the washout of intimacy. The zooming rate of divorces, separations, wife-swapping and other fun-and-games all underline an America with a leftover dream that love-conquers-all. In its place, the computer takes over sex, and a social dread of intimacy spreads to the individual's obsession with intimacy. But to know, really know, another human makes for another absurdity. Sexual intercourse, minus "sexual privates," no longer warms over the need for intimacy. If Orwell's 1984 ever turns into today, the most reliable manifestation of intimacy may be a murdered victim's final look. With his victim's face forever impinging on his psyche, the murderer would then fully appreciate the unique gift of an individual existence having been offered. An act begun in hate can end in love if self-awareness is inclusive enough to implicate another's awareness.

Such an epiphany reads like Caesar's *"et tu Brute"* —
in any case, Mailer's "dialogue with eternity" sounds
like a monologue on the probability of the Sixties
becoming 1984 before its time.

And this is what shows up in *An American Dream,*
where Mailer dramatizes his theory of violence and
the psychopath for a culture on the brink of Orwell's
nightmare future. Through Rojack's dream, Mailer
isolates one action by a psychopath on the move.
Once he commits murder, Rojack discovers that his
"forest of nerves" has a new dimension. In "trying to
create a new nervous system for himself," he relies on
"a certain instinctive wisdom" which gives him "a
radical vision of the universe." Social pressures give
way to private manners, and personal quiet gives way
to cosmic dread — and Rojack becomes Mailer's "philosophical psychopath" who can "internalize the
norm" so well that he outwits the entire Establishment. But the classic hipster has changed his spots
from an illiterate hoodlum with a knack for kicks to
an academic intellectual with a flair for magic. But
this brand-new "antithetical psychopath" still projects
the full impact of his "enormous present" — rare for a
murderer unless he keeps his "narcissistic detachment." Mailer also makes Rojack aware of the nuance
between social psychosis and private psychopathy. Rojack's dilemma settles on his attempt to transcend the
social norms which lump guiltless murderers among
the criminally insane. When he says — "There was
nothing so delicate in all the world as one's last touch
of control" (196) — he is referring to his "new nervous
system" delicately tuned to an individual on the edge
of sanity. With Rojack, Mailer may have created his
ideal psychopath, but inauthentic morality in America
makes an ideal act of violence an absurdity. As a
result, Mailer relies on the following index to an
American murder — the quantity of sanity will depend
on the quality of the violence.

In theory, Rojack's dream is structured on "con-

scious violence." It extends back to the Italian campaign during World War II when Rojack killed "four
very separate Germans" (2). His pinpoint awareness
of his first three victims has keyed him to the fourth
German who

> stood up straight with a bayonet in his hand and
> invited me to advance . . . I wanted to charge as if that
> were our contract, and held, for I could not face his
> eyes, they now contained all of it . . . those bloody
> screams that never sounded, it was all in his eyes, . . .
> and I faltered before that stare, clear as ice in the
> moonlight, and hung on one knee, not knowing if I
> could push my wound, and suddenly it was all gone,
> the clean presence of *it*, the grace, *it* had deserted me in
> the instant I hesitated and now I had no stomach to
> go. (5)

Rojack's epiphany is impure because his violence is as
authentic as a war tolerates. Alongside violence that is
usually "large scale and abstract," Rojack's wartime
act comes out isolated and intimate, but not enough
("I could not face his eyes") to give him moral energy. At best, he ends with a new self-awareness that
sticks—("Murder I had known was there for a long
time" [8]).

His killing of the Germans stays impressed on Rojack's psyche years later when his sense of "failure"
limits him to one alternative—suicide or murder. Rojack's decision to take his wife's life bears the mark of
an American Cain no longer dismissed as evil; his
recourse to violence stands for another outbreak of the
"plague" that Mailer sees in America. Beneath its
affluence and smugness, American life feeds on an
anxiety dream. All the key figures in Rojack's dream
—Deborah, Cherry, Shago, Kelly—teeter between suicide and violence. To beat the plague, one has "to
encourage the psychopath in oneself"; in this, Rojack
excels, but not enough to transform the murder of his
wife into an act of authentic violence.

When contrasted with "four very separate Germans," a wife (how much more unique can a victim get?) seems ready-made for a murder with intimacy. But Rojack admits—"My eyes were closed" (31). Again, he does not completely expose his will to his victim's reactions; instead, he exposes himself to the magic of his imagination.

> To my closed eyes Deborah's face seemed to float off from her body and stare at me in darkness. She gave one malevolent look which said: "There are dimensions to evil which reach beyond the light," and then she smiled like a milkmaid and floated away and was gone. And in the midst of that Oriental splendor of landscape, I felt the lost touch of her finger on my shoulder, radiating some faint but ineradicable pulse of detestation into the new grace. I opened my eyes. I was weary with a most honorable fatigue, and my flesh seemed new. I had not felt so nice since I was twelve. (31–32)

His epiphany—or "the new grace" locked inside—is based on fancy, not fact. Replacing moral energy is the energy of Rojack's imagination, enough to make Deborah's murder authentic in a one-man world. His crime is authentic to the extent that he can imagine its effects transcending American experience with ordinary guilt and punishment—a transcendent force that initiates him into the mysteries of dread and magic or those "dimensions to evil which reach beyond the light." Murder—since it exposes one to the nature of power and morality in the universe—endows Rojack with greater self-knowledge. To this extent, Rojack's violence is authentic.

Otherwise, Rojack's violence (like his dream) is too American. No single imagination can completely shut out the fact that to stay in America is to share its style of guilt. Once a murderer, Rojack may sense his passing into a new existence—"I was feeling good as if my life had just begun" (29)—but soon, he opens his eyes (too late) and stares at Deborah's corpse and resists "an impulse to go up to her and kick her ribs, grind

my heel on her nose, drive the point of my shoe into
her temple and kill her again, kill her good this time,
kill her right" (50). But Rojack can never fully
"right" the murder, because his eyes had shut out his
wife's death look. In darkness he fancies that American experience (the shaper of this bitch) has stolen
Deborah's final look and has locked it outside his new
life—and that American experience continues to
shape "that violent brutish tyrant who lived in Deborah" (55) until it turns the magic black and stains his
dream. Deborah's "lone green eye" that flicks on his
anxiety is the mind's eye of America locking up a
murderer. Hounded by police and pushed into a
morgue to view the body, Rojack feels "guilty for the
first time" (77). America's green-eyed power (jealous
of the guiltless) ups the pressure so much that he
almost sinks under the anxiety and almost succumbs
to "a vast cowardice . . . preparing to cry out that I
too was insane and my best ideas were poor, warped,
distorted, and injurious to others" (87). The longer
he stays in this self-made "trap," the more the black
stuff of Deborah takes over, until he imagines himself
to be a "brutish tyrant." Like one of the cops who had
"misshapen" the face of the Negro at the precinct,
Rojack works out on Shago Martin, realizing "this was
how children came to kill little cats" (193). But Shago—whose put-down of self-pity makes him a winner
—ends as a big cat with manners that transcend the
need for hatred, and Rojack senses that violence could
turn into a habit that would make him a loser. His
anxiety-dream awakens him to a new dilemma: either
fall victim to the habits of a "psycho" or establish a
pattern of authentic violence ("do it") until guilt
loses all power over him.

His encounter with Kelly (which "reek[ed] of murders still unconceived" [254]) shows Rojack the im-
possibility of resolving his dilemma in America. On
the way to the Waldorf, he imagines himself going to
Harlem, armed with Shago's umbrella, proof that he
is "the latest white man to give up the guilt" (203)—a

belief that Kelly changes into a pipe dream. Incest has been Kelly's epiphany into the nature of violence, a lesson he drives home to Rojack. One can turn American, substitute a nonviolent taboo (like incest for murder), and watch out for those few who really turn to violence and "do it" in the name of power. Or one can turn exile by testing the limit of authentic violence in America. And so Kelly dares Rojack to "do" the walk around the parapet—a violent act, unique, isolated, at the height of intimacy, with no awareness outside the self except for the magic overhead. As a symbol of America teetering between suicide and murder, Rojack walks and discovers that to divert violence from others to the self leads to a life on a tight rope, resolved by either an intentional jump or an accidental slip, doom in either case. America offers a violent individual a choice between willing one's own death (a kind of authentic suicide) or gambling one's own life (a kind of authentic murder of the self). Most Americans end up suicidal, and what passes for authentic violence turns inward, conscious only to the self. Rojack—after one trip around the parapet, done for survival on his own terms—wards off Kelly's jab with the umbrella, and "in a rage," he strikes Kelly, "across the face . . . and in relief, some relief, wrong or right, I did not know I turned and hurled the umbrella over the parapet" (260). With his refusal to add another American murder to his dream, and with Shago's umbrella (a reminder of one black American's accidental slip) gone, Rojack realizes he must flee to a jungle with its four-legged index to violence.

From Rojack's scene with Deborah's body at the morgue where "hope withered in the dialogue between the neon tube and the television set" (77)—to his dialogue with Kelly at the summit of American power, Rojack's dream has turned too American. A murder—which should have been Rojack and Deborah "engaging in a dialogue with eternity"—becomes an American monologue.

In *An American Dream*, Mailer's theory of authentic violence finds no way for American morality to come to terms with a "new nervous system" of a murderer. Murder in America results in a paradox. On the one hand, murder creates a freak, an individual too aware and sensitive and isolated, catapulted completely outside American experience; on the other hand, murder plunges an individual into the stuff that makes up the American Dream of violence, a mixed love and hate swinging between the real and the vicarious, nuances known only to the murderer who tries to "do it" at the heart of American experience. If 1984 ever comes to America, Rojack's dream will become reality, but with one exception—hipsters, White Negroes and other "philosophical psychopaths" will exit to a foreign jungle, far from the brutes stationed at the Waldorf Towers.

But Mailer ended the *Mademoiselle* interview with a surprise: "The White Negro is no longer true . . . There weren't enough White Negroes around and so the organized world took on my notion of the White Negro and killed the few of us a little further."

The "organized world's" takedown of the hipster was swift. Within months after *The White Negro*, the literary marketeers shuffled Mailer's originality and vitality into the slick and the staid. The hipster's eclipse began with Jack Kerouac's *On the Road*, which started the roadshow of the "beat generation," with its superstars, the "beatniks." With its commercial knack, the literary establishment assimilated the hipster hero into beatnik heroism. And soon, the beatnik (more the traditional bohemian, middle class, moralistic, intellectual, sentimental, hooked on zen, onanism and frigid women) took stage center, while the hipster (the unorthodox rebel, proletarian, amoral, physical, "cool," hooked on big moments with violence and sex) became a stand-in for the "beat generation," and otherwise faded out of sight.

Everywhere there are signs that Mailer has gone underground in answer to America's snub of his ideas on rebellion from the bottom. In *Cannibals and Christians*, Mailer's silence on (new and improved) revolutionary strategy tells a lot. In the wake of the beatnik's (and the "rubbed in" hipster's) eclipse, he puts forth one bittersweet gesture: "one could say the Beat Generation was a modest revolution, suicidal in the center of its passion. At its most militant it wished for immolation rather than power, it desired only to be left free enough to consume itself" (28). More recently, the beatniks have passed into the hippies whose soft (almost cute) name must make Mailer's hipsters turn over in their gray graves. Mailer's much ado about authentic violence also fades, except for a brief allusion to the war in Vietnam: "Let us, then, fight on fair grounds . . . fight like men, go in man to man against the Viet Cong. But first, call off the Air Force. They prove nothing except that America is coterminous with the Mafia. Let us win man to man or lose man to man, but let us cease pulverizing people whose faces we have never seen" (81).

With Shago Martin marked as a victim "whose face we have never seen," *An American Dream* fails to produce a White Negro undertaking a one-man revolution. Instead, a new White, Rojack, upstages Martin who "wished for immolation rather than power" and who dies, murdered, reported offstage. Rojack, who survives as a murderer (according to a strict reading of *The White Negro*) comes out as the best of all possible squares.

In his current silence, Mailer may still hope that the psychopaths (as a vanguard of minorities) will pit their revolutionary energy against the power at the social top. Under Mailer's original strategy, the "philosophical psychopaths," before acting on authentic violence, will organize the other members of the underworld. Sharing experience with taboos, all revolutionaries will unite in setting up their own "morality of the bottom, an ethical differentiation between the good and the bad in every human activity" (*ADV*,

348). If this authentic attitude in the new rebel takes root, an ideal consolidation of power in America will finally take place, directed by men sensitive to the basic fact of ethical existence—what makes action authentic is personal behavior based on moral nuances, not on behavioral patterns set down by a moralistic society.

An urgency tied to desperation shows up in Mailer's call for a cultural revolution during his debate with Ralph Ellison on "Conflict of Culture" at the University of Alaska in 1965. He has no doubt that "all minority groups in the world will win—that is the nature of the twentieth century." But what disturbs Mailer is the quality of the victory, because the "minorities are infected with the plague"; and so, the "final question of the twentieth century" becomes—

> When these minorities begin to acquire power—can they arouse themselves and purify themselves and search themselves to a point where they can create something that is more beautiful, more noble and more courageous than anything that came before them? If they can't, we are doomed.

The Jew as Literary Drop-Out

Mailer's first twenty years on the literary scene coincides with the so-called Jewish takeover of American letters. Irving Malin and Irwin Stark call this passing of the WASP control of the American imagination a "breakthrough": "For the first time in history, a large and impressively gifted group of serious American-Jewish writers has broken through the psychic barriers of the past to become an important, possibly a major reformative influence in American life and letters" (*Breakthrough*, 1). Leslie Fiedler, Alfred Kazin and others have analyzed why the new look in postwar writing is Jewish—or (in Malin's words) how "America has at long last caught up with the Jew." Put on the basis of supply and demand, America as number one world power needs what Malin (in *Breakthrough* and *Jews and Americans*) singles out as the stuff of Jewish literature: 1] a focus on "exile" or alienation; 2] a "sense of the past" or "historical memory" with its roots in the "Old Country"; 3] much ado about "the father-son relationship"; 4] the "agony of feeling" or the "theme of suffering"; 5] traditional dualities" (such as alienation / acceptance, power / humility, disbelief / faith); 6] a passion for "Transcendence"; 7] literary devices of irony, fantasy and parable. This "Jewish Experience" fits the style of America turned world leader. American manners have gone cosmopolitan, and the Jew (highly urbanized with European roots) finds himself an expert of the Establishment. The current array of Jewish writers reads like a Who's Who in American letters

—Bellow, Malamud, Roth, Gold, Salinger, Woulk, Kopit, Gelber, Shapiro, Swartz, Fiedler, Trillings, Howe, Rahv, Goodman, Heller, Friedman, Larner and many others—including Mailer.

In the beginning, Mailer and the "Jewish Experience" seem inseparable, not surprising in a writer who admits he grew up in "the most secure Jewish environment in America" (*Current Biography*, 1948). But *The Naked and the Dead*, with its treatment of the Jew, shows the Jewish roots in Mailer coming to the surface, exposed and insecure. To make up for the absentee Negro on Anopopei, the targets of bigotry are Jews, Goldstein and Roth. Their chief tormentor is Red Gallagher, whose Catholic Boston background and Rightist politics swell into anti-Semitism. Except for Martinez and Ridges, the other soldiers, through indifference more than hatred, usually aid Gallagher's bigotry.

Of his twin targets Joey Goldstein is more ready-made. A Jew from an orthodox household, he bulges with Hebraic tradition, and turns hypersensitive when ridiculed by the "Anti-Semiten." Usually he responds by feeling a mixture of inept anger and self-pity that soon gives way to his innate "warmth and simplicity" and his intense desire for solid friendships. "Essentially he was an active man, a positive man" (448). The source for his energetic optimism shows up in Goldstein's "Time Machine" (what Malin includes in *Breakthrough*) which features the old man Mosher Sefardnick who imparts his Talmudic wisdom to his grandson, Joey. After rejecting any Judaic uniqueness as a race, creed or nation, the patriarch settles on a psychological definition: "Yehadah Halevy said Israel is the heart of all nations . . . And the heart is also the conscience, which suffers for the sins of the nations . . . We have suffered so much that we know how to endure" (483). It is this belief that later inspires Goldstein to outlast the weaker Gentiles, Stanley and Brown, while matching the stamina and courage of the stronger Ridges, in their futile attempt at preserving Wilson's life and body. Even after the delirious Wilson coughs out, "Y' goddam Jewboy" (667), Goldstein nourishes his spirit with echoes of his grandfather's Israel: " 'Israel is the heart of all nations.' . . . it was the heart that suffered whenever any part of the body was ill. And Wilson was the heart now" (672). At the end, Goldstein, a Jew, shares with Ridges, a Gentile, a common sadness over a dead comrade and "the origins of a vast hopelessness" (682). With Goldstein Mailer works in a microcosmic Israel in a Jewish soldier who learns "how to endure."

Compared with the keyed-up Goldstein, Roth (Mailer's other Jewish soldier) is "so slow, so solemn" (476), and he condemns Goldstein's gushy Jewishness. Trained by modern parents, agnostic Roth sees an orthodix cultist as a throwback to "old wives tales" (54). His educated mind and aloof disposition bar him from normal conversations with the others, except for the clannish Goldstein. Throughout the novel, their discussions give the young Mailer an opportunity to dramatize the Jewish question—should Judaism be preserved and kept distinct (Goldstein's view) or should it be assimilated and made extinct? "I have never detected any similarities in Jews. I consider myself an American," (476) proclaims Roth. But this militant attitude brings only an acute sense of failure, urging him to withdraw from Jew and Gentile alike. From such a nadir Mailer restores Roth to thematic heights equal to Goldstein's. The apathetic Roth suddenly becomes a man of feeling, while soothing a crippled bird (529). Once his basic sensitivity flares up, Roth is pressured into a self-discovery which almost overpowers him during the climb up Mount Anaka. All his inner purpose has collapsed and, in his present hopelessness, only Gallagher's slap and "Get up, you Jew bastard" can arouse him: "It's ridiculous, thought Roth in the core of his brain, it's not a race, it's not a nation. If you don't believe in the religion, then why are you one?" (661). Goldstein's cult of suffering—Judaism's sentimental communion with mankind—turns out absurd. What is substituted is feeling directed inward, what Mailer terms "a magnificent anger" (662). It enables Roth to transcend his former self-pity and become "alone in the new rage of his person" (662). Seconds before falling to his death, Roth feels "contempt," and sees Gallagher as "a frightened bully—and Roth knew suddenly that he could fact Croft" (665). This sudden self-awareness invests his death with resolution and dignity.

Roth's martyrdom on Mount Anaka compares with Goldstein's endurance in the jungle. In fact, Mailer's two Jewish characters end up much more humane than his Gentile characters. The superiority of Roth (in intellect) and Goldstein (in spirit) runs on their rapport with humanistic values during wartime, rooted in Jewish strength hardened through loss and pain.

But the real introduction of the upbeat Jew (as tops in humanity at war) occurs in "A Calculus at Heaven," its Jewish figure an adolescent's preview of Goldstein and Roth. Next to the Jews on Anopopei, Wexler sticks out as a complete grotesque. Minus the big nose, he is "the biggest toughest blond Jewboy ever to play football for Freehold High" (ADV. 53). The sentimentality thickens as Wexler reconnoitres the enemy (as if scoring a touchdown against the Gentile Establishment) before he dies, machine-gunned while tossing an imaginary forward pass. Such mawkishness—by which instant Jews pass for ideals of Gentile heroism—is not found in Roth and Goldstein who are, at least, Jewish stereotypes who make it on their own.

Mailer's passing from Wexler (tied to the Goy) to Roth and Goldstein reads like a choice of stereotypes leading nowhere, and (in retrospect) the signs are clear-cut that the fictional Jew for Mailer is a dead

end. Roth and Goldstein, despite their wartime prom-
inence, have Jewish traits that the later Mailer will
either discard or despise. Both want to fit in the American scene (home, family, job), but their obsession
with their Jewishness makes them rootless and marks
them as outcasts; and worse, they compensate (as
Jewish Sad Sacks) by compulsively seeking personal
security through social acceptance. Both excel at suffering, are experts at self-pity. These traits (future
castoffs) suggest that Mailer is exhausting (not exploring) all his possibilities of tuning the Jewish character to a strategy that should engage a Jewish writer.
The Naked and the Dead marks the beginning of the
end of the "Jewish Experience" in Mailer's fiction.

Between 1948 and 1963, Mailer's direction takes
him further from his Hebraic roots, as the "Jewish
Experience" continues to fade from his fiction and
essays, either ignored, or (at best) reduced to minor
comedy. Jewishness drops-out in *Barbary Shore*—surprising, since critics usually tag it as a throwback to
the proletarian novel of the Thirties, which usually
featured Jewish intellectuals on the move for Marx.
But there is nothing Jewish about Mailer's second
novel. Almost the same is true of "The Man Who
Studied Yoga" except for Sam's half-hearted reverie as
"quarter-Jew . . . the Jew through accident, through
state of mind" (*ADV.* 185). Besides lumping Judaism
with other stand-by religions, Mailer identifies it with
stagnant middle-class minds. Its catchall style in Sam
Slovoda, a sympathetic comic butt, hints at Mailer's
further rejection of the Jew as a serious protagonist.
His snub of the Jew carries to *The Deer Park*. Supposedly Hollywood suffers Jewish control, but Mailer ignores this matter. Except for off-stage characteristics
—such as Collie Munshin's name or his speech
mannerisms—Mailer makes his Hollywood cast as
non-Jewish as possible. Even when Herman Teppis
rationalizes his dirty acts with phoney religious and
ethical beliefs, the god and code conjured up belong

to the faceless middle-class. Later, Mailer creates a Jewish girl who conceivably could be one of Teppis' turned-on granddaughters.

Denise Gondelman, the arrogant Jewess in "The Time of Her Time," highlights Mailer's fall out with the Jew. Denise enters, a self-conscious Jewess, a show-piece of American neurosis—"She was enthusiastic about her analyst, he was also Jewish (they were working now on Jewish self-hatred), he was really an inte-grated guy" (ADV. 489). Again, the Jew falls into step with standardized mentality and established mo-rality. O'Shaugnessy, the hipster-in-training, labels Denise "square." And Mailer seems to agree, by por-traying a bogus Irishman victimizing a socially ap-proved Jewish girl. O'Shaugnessy's avenging "tool" amounts to sexual and cultural superiority, while the Jew ends up an also-ran. Mailer lets his Goy narrator single out the Jew at odds with sex: "There was a Jewish tolerance for the expected failure of the flesh" (493). The Gentile remains a top pro alongside De-nise's other lover—"a very nice guy, passive Arthur with his Jewish bonanzas of mouth-love" (499). This Jewish failure at sex hints its peak at that triumphant moment when O'Shaugnessy, during his anal assault, jars Denise into her first genuine orgasm with: "You dirty little Jew" (502)—an eleven year echo of Roth's exposure to that same verbal shock, which had spurred a Jew into greater manhood, a self-awareness that made him feel superior to the Gentile before his death. Now a Jewess (pushed by anti-Semitism) comes upon sexual fulfillment. Less the weak Jewess, and more the strong woman, Denise has clearly im-proved. O'Shaugnessy concludes: "And like a real killer, she did not look back and was out the door before I could rise to tell her that she was a hero fit for me" (503). But the creator is paying homage to his creation. Later Denise will go on to subjugate Arthur and other inept males, but all her sexual conquests will be dampened by a memory of her submitting to a Gentile who forced her initiation into womanhood.

Unlike Roth, a self-created man, Denise remains an other-created woman.

In its non-fiction *Advertisements* also reveals how Mailer has shelved his Jewish heritage. The Jew drops out in *The White Negro*, not even worth an honorable mention in Mailer's strategy of a rebellion by minorities. But it is in Mailer's "muted autobiography" where "Jewish Experience" makes its most conspicuous exit. Mailer as Jew never appears in those italicized sections, otherwise singled out for their frankness. Silence has never been one of Mailer's virtues. From beginning to end—from rah-rah Wexler and his tragic heroics to done-in Denise and her comic epiphany—*Advertisements* reads like a non-Jewish book by a writer who has "muted" the fact that he is a Jew.

It is in "Responses and Reactions I" (*Commentary*, Dec. 1962) where Mailer works in his capsule biography as a Jew. Even though his parents were "Orthodox, then Conservative," and though he attended a Hebrew School, Mailer immediately denies ethnic commitment. More characteristic is his: "I was a Jew out of loyalty to the underdog." At Harvard—following his movement from Brooklyn and its Jewish culture—he begins to realize: "I had less connection to the past than anyone I knew." And after surveying two hundred years of Hebraic tradition, he asserts: "I would never, no never, have been a member of the Jewish Establishment." The occasion for Mailer's résumé of his Jewish past is the start of by-monthly columns on Martin Buber's *Tales of the Hasidim*— "Responses and Reactions" which will skim over "Jewish Experience" in favor of nondenominational styles of existentialism, magic and mysticism which will shape *An American Dream* and *Cannibals and Christians*. Again Mailer refuses to be a Jewish writer: "The reactions to the *Tales of the Hasidim* will be the natural work of a non-Jewish Jew, an alienated American, an existentialist without portfolio."

In *Presidential Papers*, "a non-Jewish Jew" discusses

why the Jewish minority in America has "lost the root" (192). Mailer begins by stressing that "the average man in a minority group is no longer a member of that minority" (189). The postwar Jews (not the Negroes, who "have emerged as an embattled and disciplined minority" [187]) have shed their ethnic skins, by mimicking the Center. Hellbent on assimilation, the Jews have kept climbing from the middle to the top, until Hebraic uniqueness and self-awareness no longer color the American scene. This vanishing Jewishness has a theological basis: "The Jews . . . are obsessed in their unconscious nightmare with whether they belong to a God of righteousness or a Devil of treachery—their flight from this confrontation has rushed to produce a large part of that mechanistic jargon which now rules American life in philosophy, psychoanalysis, social action, productive process, and the arts themselves" (189–90). In recent history, the key event that triggered this decline in Jewish identity was the religious disillusionment caused by the Messiah's cool permissiveness during the genocidal rub-out in the World War II concentration camps. Unlike the American Protestants with their "several existential philosophers of importance . . . the conventional Jews in America" have become metaphysical drop-outs: "Angst is left to the mechanical formulations of the analyst who now leans less on Freud and more on Equanil" (193). Though at ease with the American Dream, the "Jewish Experience" has a slice that intrigues Mailer: The Jews' "irreducible greatness . . . found in the devil of their dialectic, which places madness next to practicality, illumination side by side with duty, and arrogance in bed with humility" (190–91).

It is this "greatness" in the more primitive Jew (faced with the "enormous present") that Mailer sifts from the American Jew (obsessed with the past and future) when he shapes the face of his protagonist in *An American Dream*. Rojack may be "half Jewish" but his dream cannot be half American, or else, Mailer's novel about murder takes on all the trappings of the "average Jew" confronted with guilt, suffering, bigotry and other "totalitarian passions" in the "social world." To make the Jew in Rojack as non-American as possible, Mailer creates a fictive world (a replica of subterranean America) where "practicality," "duty," and "humility" give way to "madness," "illumination" and "arrogance." As a result, Rojack as Jew transcends all experience of an "average" minority. Mailer elsewhere explains: "the exceptional member of any minority group feels as if he possesses God and the Devil within himself, that the taste of his own death is already in his cells, that his purchase on eternity rises and falls with the calm or cowardice of his actions. It is a life exposed to the raw living nerve of anxiety, and rare is the average Jew or Negro who can bear it for long—so the larger tendency among minorities is to manufacture a mediocre personality which is a dull replica of the white man in power" (*PP*, 188). Just as an "exceptional" Rojack adopts the manners of a murderer ("She was dead, indeed she was dead") the Jewishness in *An American Dream* goes out as it comes in. In a flash, he remembers sixteen years ago, when he had told Deborah he was "half Jewish"; and when she had asked "the other half," he had replied: "Protestant. Nothing really" (33). And there is "nothing really" Jewish about the rest of Rojack's dream, except for Barney Kelly's momentary banter near the end. His manners tuned to the top, Kelly's rapport in America includes everyone, because power consolidation in America results from an assimilation —shanty Irish Kelly, wop Ganucci, seedy Bessie— power too mongrel to have a face. In contrast are those others not yet assimilated—Shago, an exceptional Negro, and Deborah, an "exceptional Catholic" whose "detestation of Jewish Protestants and Gentile Jews was complete" (34). But Mailer's most complete inversion of the WASP ideal shows up in his protagonist, whose name sounds like the melting pot of Europe and whose idiom bears no mark of race or religion.

On the surface, Mailer's novel seems ready-made for the "Jewish Experience"—a mixed marriage, a religious murder, a half Jew killing four Germans with Dachau on his mind; even the Sergius-to-Denise-ploy —"You're a dirty little Jew"—pops in during Rojack's unorthodox seduction of Ruta—"You're a Nazi" (44)—but again, "nothing really" Jewish happens, as Rojack's super-sex remains as non-Jewish as the rest of his dream. Never once does Rojack ever directly allude to himself as a Jew. Murder turns him into a one-man minority (Jewish Protestant or Gentile Jew?) and makes for Mailer's most artful snub of the "Jewish Experience"—a half Jew as hero in a novel swept clean of all Jewishness.

The clean-sweep continues in *Cannibals and Christians,* Mailer's latest non-Jewish book. Even in his literary criticism, the Jew in Mailer never shows. But there are signs that his break with the Literary Establishment extends to the Jewish "break-through." His disgust with "the hero of moral earnestness, the hero Herzog and the hero Levin in Malamud's *A New Life*" who are "passive, timid, other-directed, pathetic, up to the nostrils in anguish" (100) implies that a key part of the "Jewish Experience" has made its "separate peace" with America and the "plague." If Jewish-American literature has sold out, it is part of the trend in minority groups to turn "average," which has caused Mailer to shift to an existential position.

A member of a minority group is—if we are to speak existentially—not a man who is a member of a category, a Negro or a Jew, but rather a man who feels his existence in a particular way. It is in the very form or context of his existence to live with two opposed notions of himself.

What characterizes a member of a minority group is

that he is forced to see himself as both exceptional and insignificant, marvelous and awful, good and evil. (77)

How this existential minority relates to the "conflict in culture" concerns Mailer in his debate with Ralph Ellison at the University of Alaska in the Spring of 1965. Again he casts off all group-tags (Jew, Negro, Catholic), and concentrates on the individual who defines himself on his own, who ends "with a psychology profoundly different than the Center." This "ego on an elevator" (a constant up and down between self-love and self-hate) singles out those who "embody conflict in culture in their own psychology." In calling himself "a one-man minority group," Mailer connects it to critics and readers with their extreme reactions to *An American Dream*, which suggests that his present conflict is more literary than cultural.

As a kind of existential minority of one on the literary scene, Mailer finds his "psychology profoundly different" from anyone (whether Jew, Negro or WASP) turning out literature at the Center. After *The Naked and the Dead* Mailer's books (when compared with Malamud's, Bellow's, Gold's, Roth's and other front runners of the Jewish "break-through") show that his "ego on an elevator" no longer runs on the "Jewish Experience." If there is an all-Jewish Mailer under wraps, waiting to surface with a big Jewish book, the Jewish minority in America must first quit its misspent youth with the plague. But what if America quits the writer as Jew? At its present rate of growth, American experience may mushroom beyond the scope of any ethnic group of writers—or, in Alfred Kazin's words:

Was it possible, these critics wondered aloud, that American life had become so de-regionalized and lacking in local color that the big power units and the big cities had preempted the American scene, along with the supple Jewish intellectuals who were at home with them? Was it possible that Norman Mailer had become the representative novelist? (*Commentary*, April, 1966)

No writer in postwar America has been as "supple" as Mailer, and if American letters again turn non-Jewish, Mailer may go back to his roots, and turn into the last American writer as Jew.

4

The Hero on the Existential Make

In Mailer's words—"Existentialism concerns precisely those areas of experience where no expert is competent." (SI) —and one of Mailer's most existential missions is a quest for a hero: someone to be emulated in terms of cultural survival. Ideally, the birth of hero and culture should coincide. But Mailer's vision of America deep in plague makes his culture seem more dead than alive. As a result, Mailer's search for a hero includes a postmortem view of his culture, conducted in an existential manner which allows for every possibility but one—there can be no expert on heroism during a time more ripe for villainy.

A sick America immediately subverts Mailer's ideal that a hero should represent the major themes of his ethos, which would mean a hero who feels at home with the "plague." To avoid this, Mailer relies on a diverse and tentative approach to heroism both in his fiction and journalism. Seldom is there any model protagonist whose values draw out the unqualified sympathy of readers. Instead, Mailer's protagonists seem as anti-heroic as heroic. Such equivocal heroism has its source in Mailer's existential beliefs. Existential man is the total of the acts which comprise his existence. At any specific moment a hero is a hero, no less and no more. But in terms of becoming, a man's existential pattern may continue or vary or even suddenly reverse itself. Possibilities are unlimited, depending on whether the individual can master his urge to fulfill himself. Will power can transform regulator into rebel, a coward into a brave man, victim into victimizer. Heroism and villainy are amoral cor-relatives rather than moral alternatives—the concept that gives Mailer's protagonists their own moral tone. Mailer further ignores traditional heroism except for his consistent belief that courage is the key attribute; to possess courage is to be potentially heroic, possibly even representative of the ethos. But Mailer's protago-nists are usually embyronic as heroes. Mailer's ideal heroism will not be expressed until he ends his intense search for a prototypic figure who represents cultural survival and a culture worthy enough to be saved.

The wartime culture in *The Naked and the Dead* is obviously unfit for ideal heroism. Much of the non-heroic is a product of Mailer's naturalism. Free will is severely curtailed on Anopopei. The wartime "fear ladder" defines heroism as a trait to be shared by certain characters in an incomplete and yet comple-mentary manner.

Among the enlisted men, Red Valsen has the high-est aptitude for becoming a standard hero. This is the gist of his continual antagonism toward Croft and all authority. After the showdown with the Sergeant, the higher power who could and would kill, Valsen feels "glad" that "he could obey orders with submission, without feeling that he must resist" (696). The "loner" has kept his courage inactive far too long. Whenever possible, he avoids enemy action—"I'm no hero" (129). Valsen's indifference also adds to his personal deterioration. His recurring—"I don't give a damn about anything" (140)—assures his exit from leadership and the will to power.

A similar distrust of emotional involvement also shows why Lieutenant Hearn cannot make it as a hero. Educated and intelligent enough to have the neces-sary leadership, Hearn instead rejects his heroic poten-tial: "To lose his inviolate freedom was to become involved again in all the wants and sores that caught up everybody about him" (79). Only Cummings' dic-tatorial challenge to his aloofness is permitted. After the General has provoked his emotional rebellion against a superior power in the cigarette episode, Hearn reflects: "The only thing to do is to get by on style" (326). Once his shallow "style" is exposed and his humiliation is apparent, Hearn begins realizing who he really is. Just as opportunistic as the General, he begins to view his new leadership of the platoon through Cummings' eyes, using his mentor's psychological "technique" to lead "his baby" (437). "Style" has only blinded him to his psychic affinities with both Cummings and Croft: "When he searched himself he was just another Croft" (580). Immediately the Sergeant senses his lieutenant's quest for power over the platoon. In the ensuing survival of the fittest, Hearn and not Croft must die. Hearn (dead or alive) can scarcely qualify as the wartime hero.

With Croft—the chief victimizer of Hearn and Valsen—Mailer almost converts the nonheroic into the heroic. Wartime enhances Croft's superiority on Anopopei. His peacetime conditioning to psychopathic killing has made him top man at the hierarchic bottom. Even Hearn admits: "Croft they would obey, for Croft satisfied their desire for hatred, encouraged it, was superior to it, and in turn exacted obedience" (506). No one can match Croft for effective leadership and active courage. His peculiar aptitude for the military ethos runs on his identification with its code, because nothing can supersede his rapport with his platoon's welfare—"For two years he had molded it, for two years his discipline had not relaxed . . . It was the nearest thing to a moral code in him" (532). Although morally and emotionally alienated from his fellow man, Croft has compensated by "intuitively" feeling his oneness with nature. And Croft's "strained" endeavor to "shape" himself by scaling Mount Anaka fails, and he "had missed some tantalizing revelation of himself." And beyond "of life" perhaps "everything" (709). Croft can only sense how close he came to uniting the forces of nature with the irrational in his being. But on Anopopei, the facts of heroism still hover above Croft, the only soldier who excels at the perverse ideals of war.

Another function of wartime is the heroism of Ridges and Goldstein in completing their mission with Wilson's body. Like Croft, Ridges can also instinctively identify with nature—" he felt the throbbing of the jungle as a part of himself . . . until flinch(ing) before the power of it" (97). Unlike the unflinching Croft, who views nature as an index of self-fulfillment, Ridges feels that nature transcends selfhood, becoming an awesome force that demonstrates "the ways of the Lord are dev'us" (671). What results is a crude stoicism. During his ordeal with the wounded Wilson, Ridges' submission to the "Taskmaster's ways" and his "retreat" into subconscious resignation sustains him as he fulfills his mission. Still, his feat is heroic. Otherwise Ridges' shortcomings as a hero are numerous, especially his lack of leadership— "out of habit he assumed that Goldstein was to make all the decisions" (669). Though he helps the Mississippi sharecropper to "complete their odyssey with success" (679), Goldstein drops out as Mailer hero. The Jewish soldier from Brooklyn is too paranoid and inept. The continual ridicule from his comrades is only partly redeemed by the respect and friendship he achieves with an illiterate Southerner. Goldstein's devotion to their "odyssey" results from his masochistic identification with "Israel (being) the heart of all nations" (682). Apart from his lone compulsive act of courage, Goldstein is far from heroic. And yet Goldstein and Ridges together embody those remnants of nobility which are still effective on Anopopei. But wars unfortunately are won by the Crofts, not the Ridgeses and Goldsteins whose nobility is almost extraneous to Anopopei, where their attempt to save one life while hundreds are dying seems as absurd as heroic. Neither the Southern "peasant" nor the Jewish outcast is an archetype of the later Mailer protagonist.

At best, Ridges and Goldstein represent a tenuous heroism which the later O'Shaugnessy and Faye and Rojack would reject as too altruistic, too sentimental, and overly destructive to the self.

Heroism on Anopopei remains part-time and half-hearted, shared in various degrees by Valsen, Hearn, Croft, Ridges and Goldstein. Nowhere (even if these heroic gestures are added together) is there any expression of Mailer's ideal heroism. *The Naked and the Dead* is a novel without a hero or a culture worthy enough to survive.

The unripe time for a hero continues in *Barbary Shore* which also concerns a culture apt to produce villains rather than heroes. The instinctual and sentimental humanitarians like Ridges and Goldstein are gone. Not even a victimizer like Croft appears. Instead victims—lesser Hearns and Valsens—pervade the book. The shift from wartime naturalism to peacetime allegory, with emphasis now on ideology rather than characterization, explains why there is so much passivity at the Brooklyn boardinghouse. This is also an outgrowth of Mailer's theme. Courageous acts by superhuman creatures would be out of place in a portrayal of mankind growing weaker as it drifts toward barbarism. The barbarians' representative, Leroy Hollingsworth, is grotesque even in antiheroic terms. As villain, Hollingsworth is a petty exploiter; at worst he is another Cummings who has yet to grow up.

The older McLeod suffers from an abject fatigue which limits his heroic tendencies. All he has left is heroic verbosity and his overdeveloped conscience (195). Personal guilt derived from his part in debasing Marxian ideals has made McLeod an emotional cripple. And anyway, he is too much a victim to be heroic. Action, vital to Mailer's form of heroism, has yielded to memories of a prior commitment to the revolution, a "dream," "an agony" (122). Then there was "the activity and activity" (241), but now, only inertia, a symptom of the unlikelihood of growth for men in general, because his chances for improvement have always coincided with mankind's. Whatever vestiges of hope revolutionary socialism still offers must be communicated to the younger generation. Stoically affirming his own doom while instilling courage and faith in Lovett enables McLeod to assume a more conventional role as sacrificial hero. An oblique allusion to McLeod's heroism occurs in Lovett's proposed novel about an "immense institution": "The book had a hero and a heroine, but they never met while they were in the institution. It was only when they escaped, each of them in separate ways and by separate methods, that they were capable of love and so could discover each other" (58). Lannie Madison, the heroine, has a reconciliation with McLeod (296). Her "escape" is through insanity; his through suicide. But keeping alive the "little object" becomes McLeod's permanent heroic act. As an expedient hero, McLeod is an inversion, for he is a distinct threat to the barbaric culture about to be established. Though villainous by barbaric standards, McLeod remains Mailer's heroic force on the other side of "Barbary."

Left behind is Mikey Lovett, the assistant of McLeod's heroism. He begins his internment at the boardinghouse "completely isolated" (19). But at the end, Lovett can feel the "shame" of McLeod's heroic defeat (288). Lovett's commitment includes much more than revolutionary socialism. It also takes on the individual's existential need to fulfill himself: "Thus the actions of people and not their sentiments make history. There was a sentence for it. 'Men enter into social and economic relations independent of their wills,' and did it not mean more than all the drums of the medicine men?" (162). To counteract determinism, individuals must reassert their wills. Unless sentiments give way to actions, the individual will find himself depersonalized and imprisoned within the mass—one of Mailer's later principles or what will make O'Shaugnessy, Faye and Rojack (on dreamtime) tick. As for Lovett, his amnesia has confined him to his "enormous present" for so long that he can only faintly relate to the future: "I'm not a brave man . . . I have no future anyway. At least I can elect to have a future. If it's short, small matter" (304). Lovett ends as a nonhero perplexed by the leftover heroism of McLeod. In the final view, *Barbary Shore* is a novel with a hero without a future.

But in *The Deer Park* Mailer's more lasting prototypes of a hero begin to take shape. Since the culture at Desert D'Or is based on distorted sensations, its most formidable members will be those who are experts in a kind of sensibility—the disparagement of sentiment in favor of the "cool." Now the rebel finally becomes a victimizer who takes wilful and direct action to realize his self. He has a kind of courage, based on an awareness that the most vital element in fear is guilt. To acquire social power the individual must train himself to feel none of the guilt which weakens people: this is the basis of Mailer's concept of the "cool." Its two chief exponents are Faye and especially O'Shaugnessy, who are foils to the "uncool" Eitel.

A latter-day McLeod, Eitel is another Mailer hero in eclipse, about to be victimized by his culture; his worst deficiency "Like most cynics he was profoundly sentimental about sex" (110). Beneath his surface sophistication Eitel allows his quest for excessive emotions to control him. His desire for sentiment borders on mania after he identifies with the revised sentimental version of "Saints and Lovers." Bobby, the call girl, bemoans the fate of her one-year-old daughter until Eitel became tearfully and "unaccountably sad." Five hundred dollars is Bobby's reward. Eitel's sentimentality resembles those gross feelings a Hollywood movie arouses in its audience, and soon Eitel can no longer distinguish between feelings legitimately his own and feelings imposed by his milieu. Toward Elena he feels a "sense of responsibility" accompanied by inner aversion—"How he hated himself"—and where is the source of his "obligation"—"the compassion was for the image in his mind. Toward the body sleeping beside him he felt nothing" (239). Sentiment has been internalized into a cultural image of himself as a Hollywood hero while Elena has been made into a celluloid heroine. Eitel's backslide to the "uncool" (from cynicism to sentimentality) best explains his artistic and political defeat and his subsequent inability to grow—"oh how I'm deteriorating" (214). An intense awareness of his decay enables Eitel to be a spokesman for Mailer's heroism while demonstrating his own shortcomings—"The essence of spirit . . . was to choose the thing which did not better one's position but made it more perilous. That was why the world he knew was poor, for it insisted morality and caution were identical. He was so completely of that world" (257). It is a world where guilt destroys and the triumphant are the guiltless. Sentimentality as much as "life has made Eitel a determinist" (368). Even though his identity as hero fades in the emotional morass at Desert D'Or, Eitel still acts as an intellectual index to the more affirmative heroism in the novel. His own ironic epitaph to his heroic career would read: "there was that law of life so cruel and so just which demanded that one must grow or else pay more for remaining the same" (346).

His erstwhile pupil, O'Shaugnessy, heeds this message and understands when his teacher maintains that "you're old enough now to do without heroes" (308). Even before his education as Mailer hero is complete, Sergius can detect Eitel's irony in his introduction to Teppis and Hollywood society "Sergius is a hero . . . he shot down four planes in a day" (63). This form of heroism is passé though it enjoys sentimental portrayal on the movie screen. Sergius instead must seek a heroism, updated, existential, that springs from the assertion of personal will. Before the "more gifted" O'Shaugnessy can claim his "extra destiny" (21), he must reject the sentimentality of Desert D'Or. And he is "cool" insofar as he struggles against self-pity as writer and man. Though finally reversing the American Dream by descending to the social bottom, O'Shaugnessy's future social power will contain no sentimental impurities to blunt his sense of victory.

Through O'Shaugnessy Mailer keeps stressing the basic difference between sentiment and sentimentality —"sentimentality is the emotional promiscuity of those who have no sentiment" (CC, 51). Mailer attacks sentimentality because it is excessive and superficial emotion. As a result, sentimentalists are too easily swayed by conventional stimuli. Society's will pulls rank on the individual's will, and the stimuli that impress the sentimentalist are invariable sacred to the culture, such as God, flag, home, mother. Of course emotions imposed from the outside are detrimental. Whether the sentimentalist actually feels patriotic is irrelevant to his emotional duty to the flag. One of Mailer's emphatic points in *The Deer Park* is that America is rapidly becoming a "sentimental land," the seat of emotional anonymity. To curtail this drift Mailer creates an O'Shaugnessy, who turns "cool" but not "cold," which would be a state of being minus all sentiment.

Faye also despises sentimentality, but he differs on what emotional character the individual should have instead. Faye has become a psychopath, which is to say "cold" rather than "cool." His experience with Paco, the Mexican drug addict, reveals his lack of sentiment; "purity," in part a freedom from guilt, is Faye's goal in refusing Paco's plea for drugs. After Paco departs, Faye theorizes: "once you knew that guilt was the cement of the world, there was nothing to it; you could own the world or spit at it. But first you had to get rid of your own guilt, and to do that you had to kill compassion. Compassion was the queen to guilt. So screw Paco, and Faye burned for that sad pimply slob" (159–60). With sentiment still counteracting his apathy, Faye tests himself on the greater taboos, hoping to make his coldness inviolate. This is what moves him to destroy Elena. As she enters his bathroom with his sleeping pills: "he sat immobile, determined not to move, not for an hour at least. He saw this as his duty to Elena for he suffered remaining in his chair" (340). After an hour Faye's psychic control breaks, before the enormity of the taboo and the audacity of his deed. At the bathroom door, "he began to sob a little" (340). Discovering Elena still alive provokes within Faye contradictory feelings—"hatred for Elena followed his relief, so intense he could have struck her to the floor" (341). And then: "Faye knew he was defeated. He could not help it—he had his drop of mercy after all" (341).

As hero, Faye's failure is mainly one of style. Mailer would agree with Faye's obsession with courage, action, growth, and with the fact that he victimizes the moral phonies at Desert D'Or. But he never figures out what he most needs—"a point of the compass, any point, and he could follow it on some black heroic safari" (328). The "point" (to be "cool") never gets made and his quest for self-fulfillment lapses into self-destruction. "Everybody's scared" (333)—so believes Faye (as does Mailer) but the way he combats his fear is overdone. Faye's anxiety is so great that it impairs his ideal role as Mailer hero overthrowing a villainous culture. Almost a decade will pass before the standard psychopath gives way to the "philosophical psychopath," when Mailer adapts the style of Faye to the dream of Rojack. In the meantime, the "sentimental land" (minus O'Shaugnessy and Faye) still thrives, with chances for America's survival that much less.

Following *The Deer Park* Mailer's search for a hero shifts to the hipsterism of *The White Negro*. As expected, a chief means to promote growth is to be "cool." In the Hip context, to be "cool" means "to be in control of a situation because you have swung where the Square has not, or because you have allowed to come to consciousness a pain, a guilt, a shame or a desire which the other has not had the courage to face" (ADV. 352). Here O'Shaugnessy's "coolness" appears largely unchanged, except for a new emphasis on the struggle between the sentimental Square and the sensitive Hip, in which the hipster usually gains "control" because he is "equipped" with more courage. A takeover of courage makes the hipster a militant rebel threatening the cultural establishment. Alienated, and considered by Squares to be a demonic antihero, the hipster for a while becomes Mailer's preserver of selfhood.

The rebellious energy in the hipster's image slackens in *The Presidential Papers*, a result of American conformity which has fostered a further decline in romantic individualism. America has turned "too Beat," and the hipster as satanic hero has faded in a culture whose later fad is the "horde" of Beatniks—"heroes none, saints all" (41). In desperation, Mailer looks for a hero among public figures.

Heroism goes national, as Mailer labels John F. Kennedy "The Hipster as Presidential Candidate," because Kennedy has traits of a "Sergius O'Shaugnessy born rich" (44). Youth, war heroism, intellect, wit, a "cool grace" are what make Kennedy the best bet to be America's hero. This also fits the book's thesis—"existential politics": "Existential politics is rooted in the concept of the hero, it would argue that the hero is the one kind of man who *never* develops by accident, that a hero is a consecutive set of brave and witty self-creations" (6). *"Never"* accents Mailer's disbelief in chance or determinism and his commitment to existential freedom. The need for a national hero stems from the idea that state authority should also be individualized—"Power without a face is the disease of the state" (6). Cancerous America with its hectic materialism consumes its heroes in a fickle manner. Rather, Mailer would propose, "He-

roes should enter the mind modestly and go deep.
That way legends develop naturally. They come forth
over the years" (*Esquire*, Dec. 1962). Why America
keeps "cashing in" its heroes and legends is a result of
its lost heritage of beliefs which held "that each of us
was born to be free, to wander, to have adventure and
to grow on the waves of the violent, the perfumed,
and the unexpected" (*PP*, 39). These beliefs have
gone "underground," becoming a "subterranean river"
always threatening to take over the national psyche.
In such a crucial phase: "It was a hero America
needed, a hero central to his time, a man whose personality might suggest contradictions and mysteries
which could reach into the alienated circuits of the
underground, because only a hero can capture the
secret imagination of a people, and so be good for the
vitality of his nation; a hero embodies the fantasy and
so allows each private mind the liberty to consider its
fantasy and find a way to grow" (41–42).

Mailer's dream of an artist as national leader turned
nightmare when President Kennedy was assassinated.
America immediately became a void: "Now the best
heroes were—in the sense of the Renaissance—mindless: Y. S. Tittle, John Glenn, Tracy, Smiling Jack;
the passionate artists were out on the hot rods" (*CC*,
29). One not-so-passionate candidate for hero remained—Bobby Kennedy whom Mailer called "the
only liberal" not "bankrupt of charisma" (29). But
Mailer's recourse to Robert Kennedy seemed half-
hearted, since a copy (even a stand-in brother) is
always less authentic than the original. John F. Kennedy's passing from the national scene forced Mailer
to shift his quest from existential politics to existential
literature. The President's death caused the birth of
Rojack as a make-shift hero.

How Mailer assimilates the Kennedy ideal to the
heroism of Rojack takes place outside the main
"Arena" in *Cannibals and Christians*, in "The Leading Man: A Review of J. F. K.: *The Man and the*

Myth," written "about twelve weeks before Jack Kennedy took his visit to Dallas" and four weeks before "work was begun on *An American Dream*" (173). Jack Kennedy is so much a "new kind of political leader" that he becomes "a metaphor. Which is to say that Jack Kennedy is more like a hero of uncertain moral grandeur: is his ultimate nature tragic or epic? Is he a leading man or America's brother?" (168). As a "metaphor" of America, Kennedy is cast in a more existential role—a leader who transcends the cultural norms of good and evil, of heroism and villainy, who becomes one without any preconceived nature or "a Kierkegaardian hero": "Kierkegaard had divined that there was probably no anguish on heaven or earth so awful as the inability to create one's nature by daring, exceptional, forbidden, or socially impossible acts" (169). Mailer then explains the metaphorical relation between hero and culture: "We had become a Kierkegaardian nation. In the deep mills of our crossed desires, in the darkening ambiguities of our historic role, we could know no longer whether we were good or evil as an historic force . . . we needed to discover ourselves by an exploration through our ambiguity" (170). Mailer is already describing Kennedy and America in heroic terms that will later fit Rojack. In the meantime, Kennedy's death in November of 1963—which transformed him into a historical symbol rather than an existential metaphor—deadens America so much that one of its noisiest spokesmen suddenly loses his voice. Nowhere in *Cannibals and Christians* does Mailer directly express his feelings toward Kennedy's death. But everywhere in Rojack's characterization there is a hint of Mailer's attempt to resurrect Kennedy as a hero who belongs more in a novel than in America.

Rojack's opening words—"I met Jack Kennedy in November, 1946"—can almost read, in terms of how Mailer has conceived him—"Jack Kennedy became me in November, 1963." This is not to say that the parallels between Kennedy and Rojack are obvious and real as much as implicit and ideal. Still obsessed with Kennedy's crucial flaw, lack of an imagination, Mailer creates a hero with a superhuman imagination, whose whole dream, in one sense, results from an exercise of pure imagination. Equally imaginative is Mailer's nickname for his hero—"Raw-Jock" which sounds like Raw Jack. And that is exactly the point—Rojack is meant to be a kind of Jack Kennedy in the raw: "I looked down the abyss on the first night I killed: four men, four very separate Germans, dead under a full moon—whereas Jack, for all I know, never saw the abyss" (2). As novelist, Mailer has turned history into magic, with John F. Kennedy idealized as a Mailer hero with an eye and a knack for America's abyss.

Besides Kennedy, the other force that shapes Rojack is the way Mailer identifies with the literary scene. As a kind of critic in the raw, he creates a hero, contrary to whatever passes for current heroism in the literary mainstream: "the hero of moral earnestness, the hero Herzog and the hero Levin in Malamud's *A New Life* . . . passive, timid, other-directed, pathetic, up to the nostrils in anguish: the world is stronger than they are; suicide calls" (CC, 100). Instead of "other-directed" suicide, Rojack hearkens to "inner-directed" murder. This also allows Mailer to stress the relationship between hero and courage. Again the source is literary. On Hemingway, Mailer says—"There are two kinds of brave men: those who are brave by the grace of nature, and those who are brave by an act of will" (159). The latter explains in what manner Hemingway lived, a carry over of the "personal torture" that gives substance to Rojack's dream. The Hemingway influence also shows up in the Skellings Interview where Mailer talks about middle-age (when a reader "really enjoys Hemingway") and about Rojack being middle-aged, ripe for "that attack on masculinity that comes about the time when life is chipped away." At forty-four, Rojack starts his dream when his life has already "chipped away." With his wartime heroism more a result of bravery "by the grace of nature," Rojack is initiated into testing how much and how long he can "expend" his will (*AD*, 79). The basic strategy for Rojack's ordeal is what Mailer terms an "anxiety dream" which constantly examines "how much anxiety can you take" (SI). The stations of Rojack's dream consist of a series of psychic gymnastics done in the name of sanity, in which Rojack talks more to himself than to his reader. As his own psychiatrist, he learns that murder will lead to madness unless cowardice gives way to courage. His compulsion to be the most brave when confronted by the most dread is the key to self-control. Pressures exerted by agents of society increase, until Rojack (on the brink of lunacy) fully realizes that "there was nothing so delicate in all the world as one's last touch of control" (*AD*, 196). At such moments, Rojack adheres even more to the iron law of a Mailer hero—"That which you fear most is what you must do" (203). In the Hemingway manner, the "grace of nature" lies so far outside Rojack's dream that survival as murderer depends on the grace of self.

A self-contained dream may seem too foreign to bear the name, American, even though this is a novel which alludes to the national scene and whose hero bears the mark of Kennedy, Hemingway, and even receives moonlit regards from Marilyn Monroe. But Mailer sees Rojack as a native reminder that suicide is calling throughout the "sentimental land": "Hemingway and Monroe. Pass lightly over their names. They were two people in America most beautiful to us" (*PP*, 103). At Dallas, murder called Kennedy, and America had grown too ugly for Mailer to make an ordinary hero to protest the dying of a culture. As a token of national mourning, Rojack's rebellion has meaning for America only as total inversion—dream as nightmare, murder as an act of creation, and villainy as heroism. Instead of redoing the underground man at odds with his culture, Mailer introduces a hero in a kind of over-ground, a flight of one man's imagination which enables him to perceive the life and death struggle underlying his culture.

To portray such a cultural overview, Mailer introduces a prefab American hero. Rojack's forty-four years include the Phi Beta Kappa, *summa cum laude*, Distinguished Service Cross, Congress, academic acclaim, television exposure, a beautiful heiress as wife, and other exceptional feats and prizes that seem copied out of a dictionary of American heroism. Before his dream begins, Rojack has exhausted all possibilities of growth provided by his culture. He is aware of his inauthentic past—"My personality was built upon a void" (7). Rojack embodies The American Dream who has "come to decide I was finally a failure" (8). And "suicide calls." At this point, Rojack conjures up his own dream to match the essence of his culture. Since America is still the "sentimental land," he withdraws into a private reality where all sentiment is expended on the self. Rojack's "anxiety dream" enables Mailer to dramatize a hero of sensibility as a foil to the sick theatrics of the American Deer Park. As first person narrator with self-contained feeling, Mailer's hero projects external coolness as well as internal anxiety. A reader can share Rojack's immediate and intense experience while still sensing how Roberts and the rest of society must see him—as an expert in keeping "cool." In this way, Mailer underlines a paradox of the "sentimental land"—only extreme antisocial acts like murder can give an individual an intense and varied emotinal life in America. Through a murderer's dream, Mailer presents a panorama of emotiona spaced between sanity and insanity, all extremes of hate, love, pain, even joy.

To become an expert of sensibility is to be a saint in a Kierkegaardian nation when popular saints take on the image of institutionalized guilt, which ignores the ultimate dilemma whether America is "good or evil as an historical force." Opposing such paper saints, Mailer creates his own "leading man." Like the Kierkegaardian Abraham filled with "fear and trembling," Rojack undergoes similar anguish when he decides to reconstruct his nervous system at the expense of public morality. But America is also Kierkegaardian toward murder. To commit murder is a heinous crime, but to describe murder is a Madison Avenue virtue. The vicarious pleasure America derives from its mass media's obsession with murder and violence is immeasurable. For this reason, Rojack becomes the murderer as saint, because his dream represents America's need "to discover (itself) by an exploration through (its) ambiguity." Rojack, as national pilgrim, undertakes a quest to discover all the possibilities of good and evil inherent in murder. The anguish he suffers is sacrificial in the sense that America's guilt toward murder must be purged. Rojack's role as "minor saint" is sharpened when he encounters Barney Kelly, a "little devil." "Deliver me from all this, O Lord" (250) cries Kelly, as he describes how his "fear and trembling" has caused his allegiance to the powers of darkness in America. Rojack's temptation at Kelly's hands is also America's. Murder, incest, orgy, sodomy are the marrow of Kierkegaardian experience, and the real issue is whether devils or saints will determine America's moral character at its abyss.

With Rojack, Mailer has virtually stationed his hero outside practical American experience. His hero's new frontier cannot be located on the American map; nor can it be realized in America's newest dream of conquest of outer space. Rojack's terrain, instead, is psychic. His is a frontier of a one-man consciousness at grips with ambiguities which, when acted out, become meta-cultural. Murder isolates him. Through America's eyes, Rojack's superhuman feats of courage and strength may seem like absurd heroics, but through Mailer's eyes, they are an ironic reminder that, in America, failure as a murderer is but a step away from success as a suicide. Rojack may get away with murder but America remains as suicidal as ever. Hero and culture have diverged too much. Rojack's "anxiety dream" prompts a new awareness: "I felt as if I had crossed a chasm of time and was some new breed of man" (81). Near the end of his American career as murderer, Rojack (who has gone West to "the arid empty wild blind deserts") can still say: "I was part of a new breed" (269). But not for long. Rojack's flight from Las Vegas to Central America suggests that his dream has progressed beyond the limits of American experience. With Cherry metamorphosed into a spook, with Deidre (his last link with the "sentimental land") left behind, Rojack has become too "new" a breed, whose future lies in a jungle where magic and murder seem less foreign. As a metaphor of America, Rojack ends as a sub-culture with no workable roots in national reality.

Rojack's heroism shows that Mailer's quest for a hero ideal in America borders on desperation. Mailer's disgust with America—its mood of suicide and its dead end heroes—is so great that Rojack's mode of heroism questions the feasibility of America's survival. Rojack has become an expert in murder and, in the process, has turned into a murderer of his culture. Neither "Cannibal" nor "Christian," Rojack as Mailer hero is a kind of romantic and transcendental lion in a jungle awaiting to be emulated in terms of America's destruction.

"The Roots of Things"

Mailer's style of revolution "making a revolution in the consciousness of our time" (ADV, 17) coincides with Wilhelm Reich's: "The word revolutionary in this book, as in other sex-economic writings, does not mean the use of dynamite, but the use of truth . . . that is, *of going to the roots of things*" (*The Sexual Revolution*). Both the "roots" and the "things" in Mailer's thought make up a kind of philosophy on the run. Once Mailer takes on the role of philosopher, he turns impressionistic and eclectic, with a bag filled with free-swinging terms. Existentialism is the term Mailer uses to tie up his ideology—a throwback to the overnight success of *The Naked and the Dead*— "Willy-nilly I had had existentialism forced upon me" (ADV, 93). Describing his insecure condition as a literary celebrity, Mailer says that "this was an experience without a name" and the name he eventually found that best expressed his life and art was existentialism.

As expected, Mailer's key premise stresses existence rather than essence. He affirms the individual's state of becoming, not his state of being. Any belief in a preconceived essence which may innately determine individual development gives way to a view that each man's experience is subject only to the peculiar rules of his own development. To understand his experience an individual must undergo an intense commitment to life. Involvement with the world makes it, so long as the individual realizes that his inner self is all the world possible to know. Mailer also agrees with the orthodox existentialists in asserting that human reason has no priority for apprehending truth. Besides intellect, the existential man must rely on the irrational as an empirical guide. Rivaling his rational drives in importance are actions based on anxiety, guilt, the will to power and other more primitive impulses. In Mailer's existential mode, there is much ado about existential man living up to his instinctual nature. Living in the "enormous present" of intense emotional experiences leads to self-awareness. Realization of selfhood comes about not through detached thought but through decisive and committed action. Its corollary is man's existential right to determine his own moral development. A constant exposure to moral choices brings on anxiety, especially if the individual faces a decision which turns on violating laws. If he is forced into some extreme dilemma—such as either committing murder or losing his identity—the amount of anxiety hanging on his choice may be overwhelming (the "repugnance" of Marion Faye); and for Stephen Rojack, an "anxiety dream" becomes his (and the novel's) sole reality.

Another common existential idea that marks Mailer's fiction is alienation. A cerebral approach to existence (in the style of the computer) keeps alienating man in various degrees, from God, from nature, from society and from himself. This last stage of alienation —man, godless, overcivilized, asocial, whose final rapport lies entirely within himself—most fascinates Mailer. Protagonists like Rojack, Faye, O'Shaugnessy and Lovett struggle most against total alienation—because—to be alienated from oneself is to lose the instinct to survive. It is that belief that prompts Mailer to explore the "roots" of violence, murder, suicide and other "things" that show the stuff of alienation to be emotion turned off. Mailer's answer to an age bent on the overkill of feeling is neo-primitivism, a belief that modern man should return to a more simplified and more natural existence.

This becomes a code of White Negroism and existential heroism: "To be an esistentialist, one must be able to feel oneself" (*ADV*, 341). Since the regimented others turn on to sentimentality, one must cut down others' feeling—becoming "cool"—in order to rediscover feelings unique to "oneself." Because intuition tends to resist external control, the individual's ready-made means "to create a new nervous system for (him) self" is through his senses. The intuitive grasp of experience leads to "an absolute relativity where there are no truths other than the isolated truths of what each observer feels at each instant of his existence" (354). This "enormous present" underlines the truth that the "only Hip morality . . . is to do what one feels whenever and wherever it is possible." At the "roots" of Mailer's affirmation of the senses is his belief "that the unconscious . . . has an enormous teleological sense, that it moves toward a goal, that it has a real sense of what is happening to one's being at each given moment" (386). Such faith in intuitive man is an upshot of man's alienation from his own nature, so conclusive that Mailer warns that "What is at stake in the twentieth century is . . . the peril that they will extinguish the animal in us" (*PP*, 200). Architecture in the twentieth century reflects man's passing into an animal graveyard of the senses—"Beware: the ultimate promise of modern architecture is collective sightlessness for the species" (*CC*, 240). In his "hypercivilization," man buries himself with "architecture of an empty promiscuous panorama where no one can distinguish between hospitals and housing projects, factories and colleges, concert halls, civic centers, and airport terminals?" (234). At its "roots," architecture shows man to be alienated from his sense of time and space. "Not only from his past, but from his planet" (235). Mailer's "hunt for the sign of the plague in the diseases of form" (233) leads to a vision of future "cities higher than mountains, cities with room for 400,000,000 to live" (235)—a vision that might revolutionize "the perspective of twentieth-century man": "Would the fatal monotony of mass culture dissolve a hint before the quiet swaying of a great and vertical city?" (237).

In the story, "The Killer" (CC, 233–37), this "final monotony" rides on the narrator's voice. On the eve of his second parole, a convict (an unnamed "I") experiences a vast "emptiness"—a no man's land both inside and outside the walls. America has become a vast prison where everyone is a lifer "playing prison as if it is their life, the only one they are going to have" (225). The "killer"—in Mailer's view—is the "plague"; the "I," a "diseased form," a disembodied everyman who has lost the power of feeling, a sense of freedom, and all hope. His burnt-out tone echoes America's golden mean—"By normal I mean normal in prison, no more" (226). And when paroled, what will he find on the outside?—"In the prison vistas of urban renewal, the violence travels from without to within, there is no wit" (234).

This is the landscape that Stephen Rojack transcends when he does his best to "Trust in the authority of his senses" (AD, 203). The convict's "nightmare" in prison becomes a dream outside the confines of American experience where to-kill-or-be-killed separates outsiders from insiders. In Rojack's one-man prison, a "hypercivilized" America turns into a primitive wilderness flashed to a mind no longer able to keep up with a body. His act of murder runs on impulse—"my body was speaking faster than my brain" (30). Once Rojack turns murderer, Mailer dramatizes the "teleological sense" of the unconscious —"that the messages of one's experience are continually saying, 'Things are getting better,' or 'Things are getting worse. For me. For that one. For my future, for my past, mmm?' It is with this thing that they move, that they grope forward—this navigator at the seat of their being" (386). This "messenger" keeps communing with the "harbor of his calm" (38), and "things" get "better" or "worse" for Rojack, depending on whether he obeys his instinct or his intellect.

Usually instinct prevails, because the substance of Rojack's dream is so sensuous that a kind of synesthesia results. Colors are almost heard, sounds almost seen, odors almost tasted—all sensation grows so tangible that Rojack cannot tell whether the senses represent the condition of the body, the state of the mind, or the nature of the soul—the gist of his "anxiety dream." Here Mailer tries to avoid what most other writers must do in order to communicate their fiction —an overuse of the sense of sight. What Rojack smells, hears, tastes or touches is as significant as what he sees—Mailer's attempt to equalize the senses to make sensation uniform, enough to be a more powerful "navigator" than Rojack's *summa cum laude* and the rest of his oversized intellect.

In tow with his unconscious, Rojack senses a return to nineteenth-century America when "some first trains" sounded on the "prairie": " 'Beware,' said the sound. 'Freeze in your route. Behind this machine comes a century of maniacs and a heat which looks to consume the earth.' What a rustling those first animals must have known" (131). But to be "navigated" back to a time when American life was more simple and natural is to find oneself alienated from the twentieth century which has made machines into animals and men into machines. For Rojack alone, a riot of sensation transforms America into a foreign map of an earlier time—New York looks like a faceless concrete jungle; and Deborah's Room, "the specific density of a jungle conceived by Rousseau" (21). This "quantity" of sensation—with no roots in American time or space —changes the "quality" of Rojack's experience, until he sees himself as a primitive on the loose in a land taken over by barbarians. But outside Rojack's dream, Marx's axiom works in reverse—the "quantity" of American barbarism threatens to extinguish the primitive in him. Instead of discovering (in Mailer's view) the more healthy "roots" of primitivism—a life more simple, mild and natural—Rojack finds that murder plunges him into a new life that is more complex, severe and unnatural, based on the principle of normalcy in America—"normal in prison, no more." Rojack escapes prison, realizing that America has turned too barbaric to make room for even one primitive. In the computer age, man's senses have lost all their "authority," and a man of feeling is, at best, a prisoner of anxiety. Rojack's one-way dialogue with his unconscious leads to one exit—to pass outside the "century of maniacs," to go inside the jungles of Guatemala and Yucatan where animals come first, and machines, a poor second.

At the "roots" of America's alienation from the primitive is the current style of sex, a code bent on rubbing out sensation and making man as dead as an I.B.M. Mailer sees Freudianism as the culprit at the Center; though a "genius," Freud had "answers" that "were doctrinaire, deathlike, and philosophically most dreary" (ADV, 273). With the Freudians hurrahing the Establishment, Mailer feels more at home with the Reichians. The Sexual Revolution and other works of Wilhelm Reich appeal to Mailer, who agrees with Reich's thesis that sexual potency is the criterion of mental health and that the socio-economic system determines sexual characteristics and is therefore the key to sexual health or disease.

At the vanguard of those who would make American sex more healthy, Mailer rejects autoeroticism and onanism. Orgasm, instead, should be existential and prophetic, as in The White Negro: "At bottom, the drama of the psychopath is that he seeks love. Not love as the search for a mate, but love as the search for an orgasm more apocalyptic than the one which preceded it. Orgasm is his therapy—he knows at the seed of his being that good orgasm opens his possibilities and bad orgasm imprisons him" (ADV, 347). To grow into exalted selfhood, the psychopath or hipster must explore the magnitude of his being by becoming a "sexual outlaw" (348). Increased action with sex may sharpen one's instinct and insight, depending on the style of the orgasm. A sex act which is not "apocalyptic" causes slight change in the partners, but if the individual makes it with enough "courage" to engross himself completely in the act, personal growth will occur. If everyone would take on this sex style, the sexual revolution would probably uproot America's obsession with sex that puts group welfare over individual growth. Unfortunately theory often gets lost in practice, and Mailer senses the sexual revolution passing into the clutches of American know-how—"It may be a promiscuous acceptance of sexuality" (*PP*, 133). This latter qualm has triggered Mailer's most stringent statements on sex—"Planned parenthood is an abomination" (131)—or: "The ultimate direction of masturbation always has to be insanity" (141). Mailer's rigorous tone shows he fears the sexual revolution may turn as corrupt as the revolutionary socialism in *Barbary Shore*, a fear that has made him branch off from the Americanization of Reich to a more authentic "entrance into the mysteries of murder, suicide, incest, orgy, orgasm and Time" (*ADV*, 107). *The Deer Park* ended on the edge of such "mysteries," as "the Lord himself" tells O'Shaugnessy: "Rather think of Sex as Time, and Time as the connection of new circuits" (375).

Mailer starts to make this "connection" in *An American Dream*. Narcissism leads to murder, and murder (in turn) leads to a dream-vision of the "roots" of American sex. This "new circuit" between sex and time connects Rojack to the style of the primitive who "hates feedback" or any mirror-like "observation of himself" because "it violates the natural easy functioning of his instinct" (*SI*). "Feedback" uproots privacy, and mass-media (wedded to Freudianism) keeps trying "to invade" and "to destroy existential experience." Referring to Jack Ruby's shooting of Lee Oswald, Mailer says: "We have reached that moment in history, that incredible state where a murder was actually filmed." In the near future, Mailer sees greater violations—"*Life* Goes to a Murder" or television specials on LIVE sex. Once mass-media intrudes, the "nature of the event shifts," and one engaged in murder or sex will find that "another part of (one's) personality takes over"—a part that makes one a slave of "scientific certainty" and cultural say-so.

Rojack's "feedback" comes from the moon, a symbol (as in earlier times) of the dividing-point between eternity and time. Murder isolates Rojack outside the norms of sex and time. His is a one-man's lunacy (the moon, his guide) which gives him an overview of a "century of maniacs" seeking love through pleasure. Rojack's own "circuit" between murder and sex turns him on to pleasure at its "roots"—"Something fierce for pleasure was loose" (41). "The Time of (His) Time" (disconnected from the literal and lineal) becomes psychological and lunar, and sex (under the spell of the moon) takes him on "the only true journey of knowledge . . . from the depth of one being to the heart of another" (11)—a "journey" which will lead to three women and which will end between the abodes of murderers and suicides, the jungle and the moon.

At the center of American sex stands Deborah, "a great bitch" (9), wealthy, beautiful, intelligent, an heiress of an all-American age. Rojack's nine year marriage leaves him an empty victim of the national hang-up—intense love must be total need. Deborah's "gift" of love bears one price: Rojack's whine—"probably I did not have the strength to stand alone" (18). This marital "war" climaxes when Rojack, moonstruck, suicidal, cowardly, buys the American Dream of sexual survival—the "gift" of self. As he confesses his love, he senses that "Deborah had occupied (his) center" (27). Survival calls. Deborah dies. Murder makes Rojack "fierce" to know why love and death in America are the same as sex and time.

As a "sexual outlaw," he immediately seeks pleasure for its own sake, and his ready-made object is Deborah's maid, Fraulein Ruta from Berlin. A pro from "poor European alleys," Ruta is an oversea version of Horatio Alger with a basic strategy: blackmail Kelly into marriage. Behind her "monomaniacal determination to get along in the world," Rojack comes across that part of Ruta camouflaged in America—a woman instantly at home with "heat sex . . . full of earth" (42). "Like a healthy alley cat," he makes it with "something hot and mean and greedy to take the low road" (42, 43). And they do—*fellatio*, analism, and (on higher ground) the "natural act." "You're a Nazi" (shades of O'Shaugnessy's "You're a Jew") puts her in the mood, and Rojack's Time soon comes: "and I jammed up her ass and came . . . But I had a vision immediately after of a huge city in the desert, in some desert, was it a place on the moon?" (46). Through his apocalyptic orgasm, Rojack sees American sex rooted in its own place and time—the key "circuit" btween Las Vegas (love as a gamble or a purchase) and the moon (this love's final destination). Ruta—"she was money this girl" (43)—has given him "cultural feedback" at its source.

But Rojack's present epiphany is incomplete. After making murder look like suicide, he returns to Ruta, with a "hopeless lust" to create new life—"I fired one hot fierce streak of fierce bright murder"—as Ruta climaxes—"to catch that child" (56). Then he turns "cold as ice," because his epiphany with her belongs to his past. His orgasm, a product of analism, reveals how he and Deborah played at sex in a perverse culture. The search for love—a blend of sick sex and holy money—induces men and women to practice mutual self-destruction. Suicide is the stuff of American sex. In a land honey combed with contraceptives to stamp out birth, murder (the real thing) "shifts the nature" of the sex act back to its "roots"—the creation of new life. Even Ruta, after her "Time" with a murderer, wants a child. Her "gift of body" overexposes Rojack to the destructive nature of his sexual past. Under full American "feedback," he can now kneel, cold, beside his dead wife and act out his "fierce" drama: " 'Oh, darling, oh, baby,' in that rape of one's private existence which manners demand" (60). In a nation obsessed with appearances, once murder looks like suicide, sex can look like love. Time passed with Ruta (a live German-American Dream) and Deborah (a dead one) has proved sex to be a liberating force, only if it breaks with a reality of a nightmare, and turns into a magic of a dream.

Love as magic comes with Cherry Melane. But at first, sex as survival calls to Rojack: "I wanted sex now, not for pleasure, not for love, but to work this tension" (123). And Cherry knows, because she is living out her own anxiety dream. Her "pale green circles of chronic exhaustion beneath her eyes" (89) reveal how an overload of American experience had hardened to "a sickness (that) came off her"—but "her pride would be to keep her own ills to herself, rather than pass them on" (100). Her "ills" are America's. On the surface, she glitters with "perfect clean features which find their way onto every advertisement and every billboard in the land" (61). She is the classic American blonde gone to seed, a kind of Marilyn Monroe over-the-hill but still tuned to the social bottom, which has gone to the top—the Mafia, "Daddy Warbucks" Kelly, stud Shago, and a suicide sister. Though sick with "feedback," she refuses to pass on the plague. Cherry (as her name implies) remains a kind of virgin, corrupt in body and mind, but not in soul, and only fit to have rapport with a murderer "painted with a touch of magic" (175).

Mailer elsewhere describes the "sex-as-mood" that envelops Rojack and Cherry: "The dialogue of such sex is tender, it is respectful—it respects the slow conversion of character into mood, it seeks for an artful loss of each separate identity in order to find and give life to the mood which passes from body to body" (CC, 256). Rojack finds "sex-as-mood" with Cherry ideal. Mutual honesty marks them as "explorers" outside the American nightmare, and their sex act ("cool in mood") works in magic that suspends time and place—"I was alive in some deep water below sex, some tunnel of the dream where effort was divorced at last from price" (126). Freed from cultural "feedback," he removes "that corporate rubbery obstruction" inside Cherry, and then rides to his first authentic orgasm—"I came up from my body rather than down from my mind" (128). This results in knowledge of "something about love at last?"

"Sex-as-mood" passes into love as magic, the best to be had in America during "a time which interrupts the mood of everything alive" (CC, 4). It does, in the guise of Shago and violence, and Rojack learns that the American manners of a murderer and a lover are the same. The aftermath to violence is a "broken" mood—"like all love which is spoiled we now locked together a little more" (199). Love turns into just another anxiety-dream. The magic spell—under which Rojack believes Cherry's "gift" of sanity—fades. In its place is new knowledge: "No, if one wished to be a lover, one could not find one's sanity in another. That was the iron law of romance: one took the vow to be brave" (203). Since "the root of neurosis is cowardice" (251), one must be brave before one passes on health to the opposite sex, or else, love merely multiplies the plague by two.

At her death, Cherry's "look of surprise" ends Rojack's dream-vision of American sex. From Deborah (a mind, American and cold) to Ruta (a body, foreign and hot) to Cherry (a love, magical and cool), he has experienced sex, as if he "were an observer on the moon." "You kill women"—Shago accuses—and justly, because Rojack senses that the style of sex a murderer craves takes a female back to her "root." Mailer explains: "the fact that she *can* conceive alters the existential character of her sex. It makes it deeper" but she will "sense . . . that there's something alien to the continuation of her, her species, and her family, if she uses a contraceptive" (CC, 200). Rojack's time to murder whets a female's time to create. But the plague overlaps each span of time. Cherry's first orgasm for a child sharpens her "little fever"—"I would soon be dead" (179). Even Ruta's attempt "to catch a child" makes Rojack know "the unmitigatable fact that women who have discovered the power of sex are never far from suicide" (55). To become absorbed in sex is to identify with the "power" of birth in a land whose time runs on either control or abortion. Once women sense murder taking place in their womb, they pass on to a "lonely landscape" where the moon spells out the cultural fact that "there is little which is sexual about suicide" (8). At least, murder—which "is never unsexual"—offers a "vast relief" from self-destructive "feedback" and, in turn, reveals how the primitive must have viewed himself in relation to sex —the survival of the self is a kind of magic that leads to the survival of the species.

On a desert outside Las Vegas, Rojack visits the place envisioned during his first orgasm, enters a telephone booth and, for the last time, "character changes into mood." Cherry answers, as does Marilyn Monroe who killed herself next to a bedside telephone off its hook, her do-not-disturb sign for her dream. The American Dream of sex leads to lunacy, unless murder or suicide calls. After his good-bye to American anxiety, Rojack goes to a jungle and to the real "roots" of sex—the key to the mystery of being.

Mailer's search for a "new circuit" between sex and time also settles on a mode of morality that fits modern times. At the "roots" of this "new" morality is a kind of existential theology. As "first philosopher of Hip," Mailer sees God as "not all-powerful; He exists as a warring element in a divided universe . . . Maybe we are in a sense the seed, the seed-carriers, the voyagers, the explorers, the embodiment of that embattled vision; maybe we are engaged in a heroic activity, and not a mean one" (*ADV*, 380–81). Old-time Manichaeism continues to take on the mod look in *The Presidential Papers*: "If one considers the hypothesis that God is not all powerful, indeed not the architect of Destiny, but rather, the creator of Nature, then evil becomes a record of the Devil's victories over God" (193). At the hub of such a universe, Mailer sees a conflict filled with drama: "If God and the Devil are locked in an implacable war, it might not be excessive to assume their powers are separate, God the lord of inspiration, the Devil a monumental bureaucrat of repetition" (194). Monotony and triteness bear the mark of the Devil; variety and freshness, the leftover signs of a God Who verges on Imagination embodied. Mailer's concept of goodness turns more aesthetic than moral. What his culture sets up as scientific and intellectual are ascetic in nature and represent cultural evil in its most prevalent form. Hooked on such "intellectual tranquilizers," the individual finds himself restricted to a mode of behavior, institutionalized in the name of "a deadened existence, afraid precisely of violence, cannibalism, loneliness, insanity, libidinousness, hell, perversion, and mess, because these are the states which must in some way be passed through, digested, transcended, if one is to make one's way back to life" (283). And the stage is set for a murder novel and Rojack's "way back" to salvation during a time when science remains "the only true religion Americans still have left" (*CC*, 67).

After rising from his "half sleep" beside his wife's body, Rojack peers into his bathroom mirror and asks himself—"Am I now good? Am I evil forever?" (38). Immediately he is caught up in a cosmic drama between God and the Devil, which suspends any worldly index of crime and punishment. Murder, instead, exposes him to dread, a mixture of "divine rage" and infernal fury. He becomes a microcosm of a modern Manichean war, a hopeless blur of good and evil reflected by the moon. America's moral norms turn into "mysteries." God and the Devil—sharers of magic—intervene, and set up a network of coincidences by which Rojack only encounters those few whose crimes have also "attracted the attention of the gods" (204). They bring to his dream a kaleidoscope of morality. There is Ruta whose body is a melting pot of God and *der Teufel*; and Shago, a black devil with a code of a white god. Cherry—who started out with a moral nature shared by an "angel" and a "whore" (173)—tells Rojack how "I believe God is just doing *His* best to learn from what happens to some of us" (197). Nearer the top, Kelly (the "Daddy Warbucks" of this super war) claims that he is "a solicitor for the Devil" because "Hell by now might be no worse than Las Vegas or Versailles" (236). Rojack has already seen the moral map of America turn grotesque, the "jeweled city" of Las Vegas, a heaven-in-a-hell, with the moon its glittering limbo. The neat "messages" from Christianity fade to a more primitive feel for the supernatural—"Comfortless was my religion, anxiety of the anxieties, for I believed God was not love but courage. Love came only as a reward" (204). Any reward (or punishment) eludes him. As Cherry dies, he realizes—"Now mysteries were being exchanged for other mysteries" (263). Coincidences themselves have turned coincidental for a murderer without any moral "roots." As one exposed too long to the crossfire of an existential God and Devil, Rojack decides "to be free of magic, the tongue of the Devil, the dread of the Lord" (255). At least, the mark of Cain in a jungle will have no ties with a religion of science in a land where "morality had wedded itself to surrealism" (CC, 43).

The problem of death is another "mystery" that has intrigued Mailer ever since *The Naked and the Dead*, where death is wedded to war. Red Valsen expresses what most soldiers feel when confronting death. Studying a corpse "which lay almost naked on its back" shocks Red into realizing "that a man was really a very fragile thing" (216). Usually, the soldiers' attitudes swing between acceptance and fear. Gallagher, demoralized by his wife's death in childbirth, senses the inevitability of his own death: "My number's coming." (868). The psychopathic Croft sees an "order in death" that turns even more cold and cerebral for General Cummings, who sees death in war as a mere abstraction. His journal entry about the curve of an artillery shell reads: "the curve of the death missile as well as an abstraction of the life-love impulse; it demonstrates the form of existence, and life and death are merely different points of observation on the same trajectory" (570). Mailer counters this marital blueprint with a more existential concept of death which shows up in the stretcher-bearers' task with the dying Wilson. In this episode life and death are both means to an illuminating experience, since Wilson either dead or alive remains the key to Goldstein's and Ridges' brief self-awareness—"His burden had been the vital thing. Dead, he was as much alive to them as he had ever been" (680). Death is an intimate act and condition, bringing forth a sense of the oneness of humanity. The "naked" knowledge through identification with another's death can also make an individual believe in the isolated nature and the absurd brevity of his own existence; then death becomes the present and final authority on the necessity to fulfill one's destiny here and now.

In *Barbary Shore* Mailer's treatment of death goes by default to the current barbarians. The way Lannie Madison sees the prisoners gassed in World War II concentration camps makes death an image for and a function of anonymity: "as they scratch and sob and bite each other's rind, the guards turn on the gas and roar like mad for the fools thought one would be saved and so ate each other" (213).

Mailer begins *The White Negro* with an echo of Lannie's account of the slaughter in the concentration camps. Such havoc—plus the atomic bomb—increases the chances that modern man will "die as a cipher in some vast statistical operation in which our teeth would be counted, and our hair would be saved" (ADV, 338). To avoid a death that is "unknown, unhonored, and unremarked," Mailer says that "if the fate of twentieth-century man is to live with death from adolescence to premature senescence; why then the only life-giving answer is to accept the terms of death, to live with death as immediate danger, to divorce oneself from society, to exist without roots, to set out on that uncharted journey into the rebellious imperatives of the self" (339). Later Mailer discusses death from an existential standpoint. For the mystic, existentialist, psychopath, saint, bullfighter, lover— "The common denominator for all of them is their burning consciousness of the present, exactly that incandescent consciousness which the possibilities within death has opened for them" (342). In his search for identity, an individual must set up a unique meaning for his death. He must do away with cultural euphemisms—such as "he passed away"—which serve only to alleviate the fear of death. One must also rub out the Christian belief that death is but a passing to a "heaven" or a "hell"; instead, one has a choice "to live a little more or to die a little more. And as one dies a little more, one enters a most dangerous moral condition for oneself because one starts making other people die a little more in order to stay alive oneself" (385). The preservation of energy depends on whether the individual fully sees that he is going to die. This may not eliminate the fear of death but the fear, at least, will be understood, and when it is understood, the individual may set his sights on the "roots," that death offers an individual a most exact way of defining the self—an echo of Rojack's thesis that "the perception of death" is one of the "roots" of motivation.

In *An American Dream*, Mailer's treatment of

death turns strictly existential. Death becomes a one-man show. It is only a matter of time—once killing that fourth German makes him feel "lost in a private kaleidoscope of death" (7)—before Rojack sees death as a condition that is specifically his own. Intimations of himself in the waking world—"I had lost my sense of being alive" (14)—make him ripe for a dream at its "roots," or what Mailer terms "a true dialogue with eternity" because "when we dream, we are engaged in a speculation about what our death is going to be like" (SI). A dream, at least, avoids the experience of dreamless sleep which points out in retrospect non-being. Instead, a "perception" of one's soul outside lineal, literal time (as in a dream) may also see that "death is a spectrum rather than a single final point." For this reason, Mailer believes that the manner in which one dies becomes "enormously important," because "one can become more or less afterward."

This is the gist of Rojack's "perception of death." Once he murders, his "private kaleidoscope" turns exclusively inward, a kind of "passing into death by way of going deeper to himself" (94–95). The "spectrum" of one's own death fills his dream existence with afterimages that suggest (in Mailer's words) "that time is the continuation from life into death" (CC, 362). What suspends Rojack's dream between time and eternity, between life and death rests on his inability to authenticate his "crossed impulses" between love and fear of death. As a suicide "half on the balcony, half off" (8), he lets go of "that ability of (his) soul to die in its place, take failure, go down honorably" (208). To the eye of his unconscious, his soul splits apart, its "bad" half bound to his body, its "good" half gone to the moon. Much in the style of those associational images in Mailer's "The Political Economy of Time," Rojack sees his dream of death "as sea change, voyages, metamorphoses" (CC, 328). Murder also sets loose Deborah's soul, the one death he has directly caused, which plagues him and blurs the effect of his "perception." His and Deborah's "voyages" finally converge when Kelly (a momentary "harbor" for Deborah's soul) makes Rojack's dream incandescent: "I was going to be dead in another minute; all Deborah's wrath passed now through him, he was agent to her fury and death set about me like a ringing of echoes in ether, red light and green" (253). His "spectrum" keeps flashing a kind of synesthesia of colors that never let his "perception" of his soul turn either black or white. On this "uncharted journey" to either non-being or being, his incandescent consciousness of the "enormous present" is his only guide. It lights up the clearest sense of self when Rojack decides to condemn himself to death, not like those many others who wait to be condemned. He "prepare(s) himself" as he walks with Kelly to the parapet . . . "I felt death come up like the shadow which is waiting as one slips past the first sentinels of consciousness into the islands of sleep" (256). To be "ready to die" is to be ready to live. On his way to a life in a jungle, he stops to see an autopsy on a cancer victim, its "germinated stench" (267) a final testament on how he (like most Americans) had lived and died. Death's final image, as the novel ends, belongs to the culture, because Rojack's dream under a full moon is only half complete, like waking sleep. In *An American Dream*, Mailer transforms his culture's prize euphemism to explain away death—"he fell asleep"—into an existential nightmare.

At the "roots" of Mailer's views on death, God, sex and sensation in most of his writing since *The Deer Park* is a desire to forment "a revolution in the consciousness of our time." Its origins will not be political or economic. "The next collapse in America" instead may be centered "within the superstructure of manners, morals, tastes, fashions and vogue which shape the search for love of each of us" (*ADV*, 315). Unfortunately the contemporary age is cancerous—"the despair of the twentieth century is that man's consciousness has increased at an incredible rate and yet his capacity to alter history, to make change, has never been more impotent" (324–25). If America's choice is either authoritarianism or nihilism, then nihilism must be made over into a creative force in time with what Mailer calls his "romantic idealism." As for existentialism, it is romanticism by another name, which Mailer uses as the current language for his cultural revolution. But up to a point: "I've never said seriously that I'm an existential nihilist. I think I've said it facetiously. I am guilty of having said I'm a constitutional nihilist, which is another matter. I believe all legal structures are bad, but they've got to be dissolved with art. I certainly wouldn't want to do away with all the laws overnight" (*PP*, 144). Existentialism may be the source of the word "revolution," but its basic energy only takes to art. "Dissolving" the Establishment "with art" does away with a sudden revolution. Gradualism is a better strategy, based on action through art, the "force" best equipped to replace discarded values: "Art is a force. Maybe it's the last force to stand against urban renewal, mental hygiene, the wave of the waveless future" (145). As an archrevolutionary writer, Mailer identifies with the "moral nihilists' wing" or those "more creative and adventurous" writers whose "secret belief" is that they "can save the world" by rubbing out "moral attitudes" that "do not fit reality" (*Publisher's Weekly*, March 22, 1965). At his position on "the forefront of experience," Mailer as writer chops away at America's "superstructure." His assault on diseased manners results in a novel in which manners and murder are given equal time. His overplay of Rojack's "shocking sense of smell" is his answer to a land where deodorants reign. His putting Rojack on the existential road to cannibalism, scatology, nausea and the "heart of the puke" is Mailer's way of shocking his readers into seeing their "roots" in the "modern condition": "Let me say just that the modern condition may be psychically so bleak, so

over-extended, so artificial, so plastic—plastic like sty-
rene—that studies of loneliness, silence, corruption,
scatology, abortion, monstrosity, decadence, orgy, and
death can give life, can give a sentiment of beauty"
(CC, 269). Like a Jeremiah with a missile for a Bible,
Mailer lends his own consciousness to a revolution
that continues to run on art's rapport with the taboo.

2

The Writer
out on a Historical Limb

Of Norman Mailer's first eight books, *Advertisements
For Myself* (1959) is the key to his views of the artist
or writer. It is his "muted autobiography," and judging by its various book reviewers, *Advertisements* has
become for many critical readers a kind of Book of
Revelation, a homemade Mecca for either believing or
(more usually) disbelieving Mailer's zealous cry that
his present and future work "will have the deepest
influence of any work being done by an American
novelist in these years" (17).

Advertisements, with its spotlight on a personality-
plus, has made Mailer the prime mover of what
Harvey Swados has dubbed "the cult of personality in
American letters" (*Saturday Review*, Oct. 1, 1960).
For this reason Mailer's critics snap back with surface
emotions and fall into their own "cult" of reply. Most
of the controversy centers on the book's italicized
autobiographical sections, which radiate with Mailer's
magnetic honesty, which in turn leads readers to over-
react to what Mailer is saying and to overlook how
Mailer is saying it. Mailer the man, constantly agitat-
ing his readers and critics, obscures the more important figure, Mailer the writer. Mailer's strategy (to
project one image and hold back the other) becomes
clearer once *Advertisements* is set alongside Mailer's
other scattered comments on art. Only a complete
picture will show what makes Mailer the writer tick.

The first trait that takes shape is a use of autobiography. Some of Mailer's early war experiences show up

in *The Naked and the Dead* and a few later short stories with wartime settings. Even before 1948, autobiography is the stuff of Mailer's art, because his first two unpublished novels seem to be remakes of his early life: first, Jewish life in Brooklyn; then, summertime employment at a mental hospital. What ushers in the "cult of personality" is Mailer's inability to remain an autobiographical writer. If his personal experience had remained less spectacular and more adaptable for his art, and if he had continued transforming such experience into fiction, his personality would have remained more stable. There would have been less dissociation between the man privately experiencing and the writer publicly converting his life into art. For this reason Mailer would have shunned any extreme publicity that would take the spotlight off his literary output. With notoriety out of the way, Swados' "cult of personality" instead would have been channeled into Mailer's fiction. But after 1948 Mailer's mode of art takes a new direction—alienation, deeply internalized, a result of a lopsided rate of personal and artistic growth in the same writer. For a writer to sense his personal life zooming past all understanding while his artistic life slows almost to a stop makes for a dissociation between himself and his art. Once started, it puts any autobiographical approach out of reach. The inner man has grown apart from and at the expense of the inner artist. This dissociation between the artistic and the personal in Mailer must have occurred quickly after the enormous success of *The Naked and the Dead*.

But the exact nature of Mailer as artist during 1948–51 remains a mystery, since Mailer (during those years immediately following *The Naked and the Dead*), keeps silent about the first stage of his strategy of success. Mailer's later remarks in *Advertisements* on his alienation read like a subtle manipulation of chronology. The "enormous present" of Mailer's presentation seeks to cover ten years of his past. The years

1948–51 are reappraised in the future, as if in the present. If in *Advertisements* Mailer really anticipates his own posterity (as some critics argue) then he is equally adept at consummating his past. When he describes his various psychic dislocations after 1948, he is certainly not projecting any immediate impressions. Except for comments which are pure hindsight, all of Mailer's say-so on his role as writer during 1948–51 relate to its public show, not to its private roots. Again Mailer the man pushes Mailer the writer out of sight. Already Mailer has turned into a one-man advertiser whose basic strategy will be egocentricity that attempts to pass over heads of critics.

The title—*Advertisements For Myself*—smacks of tactics of an egocentric writer. "Advertisements" and "Myself" speak for themselves. But Mailer nails down his title with "For" instead of more expected "Of." His gimmick with prepositions reveals Mailer's great care to project an ego with as much rapport with himself as with his reader—a mood created through semantics. "Of"—with its usual connotations of proceeding from, belonging or relating to, connected with, or concerning—has been junked for the more useful "For"—a semantic shift to the consideration of the view or the reference to which anything is done. With the term "Of," Mailer (the creator of the "advertisements") is the subject; with the term "For," Mailer becomes both subject and object. In this sense Mailer is writing as much for himself as for his readers. Mailer in effect is serving as his own therapist, and his reader must be alert and sensitive enough to sift the private needs from the public truths. Mailer's use of "For" also suggests that he promotes the object of "Myself" at the expense of the reader. Critics—with their "cult" of overdone replies—react to *Advertisements* as if Mailer were only a self-made subject (as if the "Of" were there); they fail to see that Mailer's "cult of personality" runs on the tactics of give and take. As an arch-careerist, Mailer pivots *Advertise-*

ments on a choice of prepositions, and "Of" with its emphasis on *concerning* gives way to "For" with its accent on *belonging*—a semantic device that makes a reader both love and hate Mailer's egotistical ways.

Advertisements For Myself, published in 1959, is a 532-page Odyssey of Mailer's first ten years as a literary figure. Its contents range from his earliest short stories to his latest work in progress. Interspersed with no respect to genre are stories, poems, fragments of plays, political and cultural essays, samplings from previous novels, reviews and interviews. To avoid a chaotic presentation, Mailer frames and threads these varied contents with a series of "advertisements" in a chronological sequence. These sections stir up most of the controversy surrounding the book; the key target, their tone. It has been characterized as naughty, perceptive, defiant, confessional, arrogant, humble, profane, candid, scatological, self-consciously filled with pity and downright dishonest. Does so much lively confusion hint at what prompted Mailer to publish his literary Odyssey at this stage of his career?

Ostensibly *Advertisements* was Mailer's attempt to acquaint readers already familiar with his more popular novels with his more obscure work. But the book's effect on the critic was calculated to serve another purpose. With his last published novel four years behind him, with nothing new to offer in the immediate future, and with his literary reputation set for an eclipse, Mailer introduced admirers and detractors alike to a new literary personality. The 1959 volume also worked out egocentricity. Grappling with his aesthetic problem by talking it out with himself while simultaneously writing it out for his audience—his way of eliminating through an intense display of ego what could otherwise remain a sentimentality that could cripple him privately—Mailer was convincing himself of the necessity for a writer to be his own worst enemy before he could become his own best friend.

The most active strategy that stems from Mailer's egocentricity is courage, synonymous with literary survival, a fact of his beginning at the top and his later attempts to stay there. Acute anxiety, resulting from "the conviction that I had burned out my talent" (332), underscores why courage has remained one of Mailer's key virtues. Its most accomplished pro in American letters, he thinks, is Ernest Hemingway: "I shared with Papa the notion, arrived at slowly in my case, that even if one dulled one's talents in the punishment of becoming a man, it was more important to be a man than a very good writer" (265). Mailer ties artistic development to personal growth, but personal fulfillment takes over literary achievement. Being a man is a prerequisite for becoming a writer. What must be prevented, however, is too slow a growth or too long a dissociation between the man's character and the artist's talent. To stop "one's talent" from being "dulled," manhood must be attained as quickly as possible, and the quickest way lies through personal courage.

With manhood just around the corner, Mailer projects to his readers a role that bristles with bold force. It is as if his literary survival were dependent on proving himself fitter than his readers. This all-out urge to compete underlies the various images that Mailer uses to make his personality more flashy. Readers are cajoled into believing him to be a "bigger hoodlum" or a "psychic outlaw" (225, 234), or a prizefighter sparring with the reader. This blend of aggressiveness and playfulness may perplex a reader, but Mailer knows the value of maintaining a courageous stance even if it leads to absurdity. Without personal survival there can be no survival as a literary force, and in the meantime Mailer keeps on shadowboxing with posterity.

Besides egocentricity and courage, Mailer is also dedicated to honesty. It is self-determined because it is based on one's intimate awareness of how equivocal all moral experience is and how absurd all modes of institutional honesty are. Truth and falsehood can flit back and forth at any moment during any action. Being honest therefore means that the self is alert to the ethical relativity in all other persons at any given time. What distinguishes honesty from dishonesty is this self-awareness, and there is a certain pride generated by recognizing one's superior consciousness. Put into the context of the courageous writer, Mailer finds that preserving an honesty toward oneself will increase strength and confidence because other people's conceit or arrogance will be based on the supposition that no one ever dares to dispel all the illusions concerning the self. Once a writer has confronted and accepted his own personal limitations, he becomes unafraid of defining the limitations in others. Such a statement as "self-pity is one of my vices" (22) can begin in weakness and end in strength. Whether a reader feels consoled or threatened remains of secondary importance to the writer whose honesty is his best method for converting personal defects into public virtues, and *Advertisements* shows Mailer to be an expert in advertising his honesty. Razzle-dazzle such as self-pitying confessions next to self-exalting arrogance runs on Mailer's willfulness. Always his mind stays in complete control. That is what is implied in his decision to "use my personality as the armature of the book" (219). The most vital single piece of protective equipment is that central consciousness which calculates the response at precisely the time the stimulus is offered to the reader. Honesty as "armature" makes for a barrage of attacks on writers, critics, publishers and even readers. Do such attacks gain enemies and lose friends? Public apathy adds up to the eclipse of any celebrity and Mailer's "armature" includes a defense against such calamity. Ardent readers or followers are pleased with either praise or indifference and seldom put out by attacks directed elsewhere. Old purchasers will continue to buy his new books. But enemies—

either made or in the making—resent everything, reading scorn into praise, responding as Mailer expects them to whenever he decides to be testy. Yet unfavorable reactions are better than no reactions, especially if a writer remembers that one's enemies are often one's most meticulous readers. Besides they still buy books. The ad that spotlights this technique of promoting popularity or even notoriety is Mailer's desire to "exhaust the emotions of others." Too bold a revelation? Too reckless? Not necessarily, since "armature" as a tactic of "personality" also works as a protection against exploiting the self with illusions of artistic and personal success. Time was when the best offense was a good defense, but to Mailer the best defense must be a good offense for a man ready to confront America with his art.

The encounter between Mailer and his milieu tells much about his strategy for the artist in public life. How a writer develops partly depends on the amount of personal identity he can retain while becoming a public figure. Egocentricity, courage and honesty must have public fulfillment or else they remain theories without force. Mailer's public image has its roots in his oft-quoted phrase: to "influence the history of my time a little bit" (*ADV*, 269). (More often than not, critics pass over the qualifying phrase "a little bit.")

A "little influence" lights up Mailer's role as literary critic, featured in *Cannibals and Christians*. America as a literary wasteland (reflected in the contemporary novel) enables Mailer to approach the work of his colleagues with mixed fear and hope. His dread that some Bellow or Styron may make it as undisputed champion of American letters matches his desire for keener competition. The Great American Novel can be written only if stimulated by the near-great. From its snap beginnings in *Advertisements* ("Evaluations —Quick and Expensive Comments on the Talent in the Room"), Mailer's literary criticism has remained "quick" and "expensive." Never is there close textual

criticism. Mailer instead prefers an incisive, witty, un-
inhibited approach, filled with imagery and metaphor
—at its best on William Burroughs' *Naked Lunch*
(CC, 116–17). Such guarded praise—Burroughs as
"the greatest writer of graffiti who ever lived"—is rare.
Usually Mailer plays at the game of critic as prizefighter. Always "quick," he usually settles for a one-round
decision. But when he strives for a knockout, criticism
gives way to sardonic spleen. Mailer's smoothest
hatchet-work takes place in "The Case Against
McCarthy: A Review of *The Group*" (133–40). As
critic, Mailer has turned self-styled destroyer.

But he can also be constructive. Although Mailer
"would rather pick up each book by itself and make
(his) connections on the fly" (113), his flights of
criticism are sometimes high, "expensive" in the sense
that they display open-minded, sharp perceptions. He
summarizes Styron's *Set This House on Fire* as "the
magnum opus of a fat spoiled rich kid who could
write like an angel about landscape and like an adolescent about people" (110). Whenever feasible, Mailer
takes to minority opinion—praising Updike's content
at the expense of his style "which is atrocious—and
smells like stale garlic." As expected, the marginal
view pinpoints Mailer's value as a literary critic.
When set against more objective and moderate criticism, Mailer's evaluations at times add that peculiar
kind of critical insight only to be had "on the fly" at
the extremes.

Thus far, Mailer makes literary criticism an
offshoot of an older, more vital concern with history
and culture. The old mixes with the new when Mailer
swings to the larger aspects of literary criticism. An
accent on the political and the social runs throughout
"The Dynamics of American Letters" (95–103), and
Mailer's preoccupation with power shows up in his
discussion of the "war at the center of American letters"—"Naturalism versus the Genteel Tradition." In
Mailer's hands, American literary history reads like a

sideshow of the Marxian class struggle. But Mailer's deep-down romance with American literature echoes in his manifesto to the American writer to do "the single great work which would clarify a nation's vision of itself" (98). Literary criticism for Mailer becomes a public platform from which a writer can assess his nation as much as himself.

As a kind of public executioner, Mailer sets his sights on the literary establishment. His attacks on it have set off the most publicity, because the critics, reviewers and publishers are just as articulate as their attacker, besides being ready-made for retaliation. The result is a notoriety in which Mailer stars as a naughty adolescent throwing dust at his elders. Identifying himself with young writers in the guise of "barbarism or decadence" (ADV, 189), Mailer pushes his attacks on the literary establishment through a colorful array of techniques. For example, he will soften the blows of detractors by making their words boomerang. On *Barbary Shore*, he advertises bits of reproductions (262) of the blackest opinions of the reviewers, but all is lightened by Mailer's bravado. His psychology is simple. The critical harm is an accomplished fact; so why not capitalize on the notion that once one has touched bottom, the only possible direction is up. Besides there is nothing more disarming than displaying one's opponents' weapon in one's own hands. What is unique in Mailer's onslaught against the literary world is how he vents his spleen. At its best Mailer's style produces a curious effect—audacity based on intimacy blended with ridicule grounded in aloofness.

Mailer's style turns moderate and his tone becomes solemn when he expresses his opposition to American culture. This includes the literary establishment and many other institutional forces out to weaken the power of the artist. This enemy's slogan is "the writer must aim to please." To be pleased is a regimented readership, its values and tastes formed by contemporary norms that pass for individual wants and needs.

Society's goals must shape the writer. National well-being takes over his allegiance, admonishing him to mature, to grow responsible and healthy enough never to question the American system. In Mailer's view, whether the writer conforms to this aesthetic norm determines whether he will take on cowardice or courage. Mailer's own choice is courage. He stands for a "literature of alienation and protest, disgust and rebellion" (188). Its agent is that artist who practices what Joyce called "silence, exile, and cunning" (190). The artist's bravery comes out as a kind of guerilla warfare against the other-directed WASP ethic, and this hostility becomes the cultural gauge by which an artist can measure the amount of courage and individuality he has. The pressure to surrender his identity to the American Establishment keeps rising until a writer must resist and retaliate even if he must adopt extreme means and ends.

The writer's greatest enemy is cultural totalitarianism which, unless checked, will transform America into a nation beyond cure through art. One of the more crucial conflicts between Mailer and the totalitarians involves literary censorship. In this controversial area, a writer's honesty (backed up with courage) takes center stage. Honesty means "to exhaust the emotions of others" on the printed page. The reader's feelings must be jarred to the utmost while he experiences the unexpected and the shocking. Invariably the honest writer exposes social taboos, especially those "do nots" concerning sex. On the literary value of sex, Mailer says: "I believe it is perhaps the last remaining frontier of the novel which has not been exhausted by the nineteenth and early twentieth century novelists" (270). A literary innovator should therefore declare his freedom from his culture's authoritarianism on sex. A writer should acknowledge his own inalienable right to pursue life, liberty and what is mistakenly labled the obscene. Those Americans at odds with Mailer's views on obscenity are duped defenders of totalitarianism. Their armor is censorship. Their base of operations is what Mailer terms "the dull mortar of our guilty society" (242). One way to combat censorship is the kind of artist's crusade for free expression "Including the rude, the obscene, and the unsayable. Art was as essential to the nation as technology" (*PP*, 91–92).

In *Cannibals and Christians*, the artist's mission in America turns symbolic. Mailer concentrates his literary opinions in Part Two, entitled "Lions," which ends with an allusion (still grounded in aesthetics) to John F. Kennedy and his "real political art." The artist, either literary or political, stands for the "lion" in the American "Arena," the foil to the "Lambs" or those duped followers of an America bended toward self-destruction. Even in a land given over to the ways of suicidal beasts, the artist still remains a potential king who could take over and reverse the drift toward cannibalism. But like Mailer's Christians and Cannibals with reversed roles, American writers usually mimick the "lambs"—by making "a separate peace," a kind of literary sell-out on the national level: "Their vision was partial, determinedly so, they say that as the first condition for trying to be great—that one must not try to save. Not souls, and not the nation" (99). Literature has "failed" to function as a mode of national survival, and America, under the tutorage of mass media, passes closer to destruction. The art of the "Cannibals" will prevail, unless literature can oust the mass media and help America to grow. This is why Mailer refuses to make his "separate peace," why he constantly seeks that "big book," that total vision which will explain America to itself.

Bits of Mailer's total vision of art fall into place in some of his fictional characters. *The Naked and the Dead* contains no character who is either an artist or a writer—a fact that may explain why autobiography passes so smoothly into the novel's texture, and may reflect how satisfied Mailer was with his creative life, enough to do away with any need to dramatize the problems of a writer. *Barbary Shore* features a writer-narrator who bears the mark of Mailer as a writer trying to survive overpowering success. His second novel introduces the tone of uncertainty and doubt; Lovett's entire past remains blurred. His past, if it included the urge to write a novel, comes alive in the literary dogmatism of Willie D. Dinsmore. The latter is a playwright who resembles "a boxer dog," frothing with anti-fascist sentiments, while yearning for the restoration of the worker's theatre because "Art is a people's fight" (10). Representing the wistful unfulfilled yesterday, Dinsmore and his literary principles signify for the young Lovett and possibly even for Mailer an oversimplified and powerless way for the artist to combat the newer totalitarianism. Moreover, Dinsmore is a week-end writer, escaping from wife, home and state. Very early in the novel he appears, expounds his opinions, and fades from the action as do his proletarian views on art. The literary and cultural gospel embodied in this character would be passé for a young writer like Mailer, struggling to keep his literary prestige with a second novel as good as his first. The artistic urge in Mikey Lovett flickers as much as Dinsmore's, for Lovett remains a daydreaming writer, whose output dribbles into notebook entries that never turn into finished manuscript. Near the end, Lovett barely remembers that "There was still the novel" (290). Far from a dedicated writer, Lovett directs his present energy toward understanding certain ideologies, especially revolutionary socialism—reminiscent of Mailer's fancy for socialism after *The Naked and the Dead*. Also Lovett's inability to write hints at Mailer's slowdown in output following an energetic fifteen months at a first novel.

Apart from *Barbary Shore*, there are other fictional artists in the Mailer canon. In one of his earliest stories, "A Calculus At Heaven," the "Artist Out of Whack" shows up in flashbacks associated with

Bowen Hilliard, a rebel artist who sells out to commercial necessity. No such surrender works on the writer portrayed in the anecdotal "The Notebook" (*ADV*, 150–53). This writer's "saintliness"—an outgrowth of his dedication to an aesthetic ideal based on exercising pure moral relativity on everything but his art—has since remained one of Mailer's vital aesthetic beliefs. "The Notebook" pinpoints what Mailer means by honesty. "The Man Who Studied Yoga" reintroduces the sellout in the character of Sam Slovoda. His half-hearted earlier attempts at writing serious novels have now degenerated into filling the narrative balloons for the comic magazines. But Sam can still feel a spark to renew the artist's crusade. Since Mailer's tonal effects in this story are complex—a blend of scornful ridicule and playful humor—the story's narrator is equally as ambiguous. And yet despite Mailer's use of a persona, an autobiographical wail sticks to the following passage, as if Mailer, disengaging himself from Sam's mind, were really describing those moments when he could sense no artistic growth within himself: "The novelist . . . must live in paranoia and seek to be one with the world; he must be terrified of experience and hungry for it; he must think himself nothing and believe he's superior to all. The feminine in his nature cries for proof he is a man; he dreams of power and is without capacity to gain it; he loves himself above all and therefore despises all that he is" (*ADV*, 184).

As a backdrop of Mailer at the crossroads of fiction and journalism from 1951 to 1955, *The Deer Park* dramatizes the conflict between creative and commercial writing. Unlike *Barbary Shore* with its lone writer, Mailer's third novel bulges with would-be artists. Located in Hollywood, the playground capital of tailormade art, various characters are contrasted with each other, each in turn reflecting a specific attitude toward art.

Sergius O'Shaugnessy—a streamlined Lovett—

represents another writer in training. Dallying with the "ambition that someday I would be a brave writer" (23), he ensnares himself in the leisure society at Desert D'Or, admitting "I hardly wrote a word while I was at the resort" (47). O'Shaugnessy first must pass unscathed through Hollywood's alluring baits of money and prestige before he can energize that "central urge" (142) to write with power. Only after his love affair with Lulu Meyers has climaxed in her vowing eternal love and fidelity, and only after realizing that a movie actress' honesty is as ethically relative as a writer's can O'Shaugnessy consider his sentimentalism (being the "patsy") to be properly dead (325). Emotionally controlled and strengthened but with his aesthetic soul intact, he can deliberately abandon the commercial trap to start his writing apprenticeship: "but I knew that finally one must do, simply do, for we act in total ignorance and yet in honest ignorance we must act, or we can never learn for we can hardly believe what we are told, we can only measure what has happened inside ourselves. So I wrote a few poor pages and gave them up and knew I would try again" (326). O'Shaugnessy must be listed among the redeemed, the dedicated.

Most of the others—Jennings James (Jay-Jay), Herman Teppis and eventually Charles Eitel—have granted allegiance to their celluloid art with its dollar ethics. Resembling both Dinsmore and Slovoda, Jay-Jay stands for another artistic rebellion ending in defeat. Once during the Depression ("the good old days" [17]), he had valiantly struggled to turn out quality stories, but recent times have only rubber-stamped his career as publicity agent for Supreme Pictures. Unlike Jay-Jay, Herman Teppis is a born Hollywood marketeer. Ironically blessed with an "instinct" nearly "infallible," H. T. dazzles his peers and turns into a rarity—"a creative movie-maker" (71). Situated between these two art merchants is the wavering Eitel with his dilemma—to be creative artist or

Hollywood craftsman. The major aesthetic problem —can an artistic talent grow or even survive when the banal environment possesses more power than the artist?—centers on Eitel's determined, though ultimately vain, attempts to preserve personal integrity and artistic merit in the otherwise crass profession of Hollywood directing. His love affair with Elena slows his drift toward a commercial solution of his dilemma, but his strength and confidence finally break down, and "the Eitel touch" reverts to an iron compromise with movies that are "tricky, dishonest and with pretensions to art" (164).

Apart from these hucksters in art stands Marion Faye, who has a special theory of art. It has nothing to do with writing novels, stories or Hollywood scripts. For Faye life itself if the most honest form of art. Its technique demands much more than acquiring life skills in order to live intensely and fully. What is more important is authenticating one's existence, always being honest with one's self during an action and never creating an illusion about a completed action. This principle remains basic to Faye's relating life to art. Anyone who aspires to be an artist but who lives inauthentically can never have Faye's respect. He "hates" Eitel, and when Eitel asks why, Faye answers: "Because you might have been an artist, and you spit on it" (184). Faye's verdict rings true when Eitel finally gives in to the Hollywood standard of art. In Faye's opinion, and probably Mailer's, creative talent can survive in a hostile environment only if the artist retains enough courage and honesty and keeps his personal and aesthetic ego insulated from everything but his creative work. At the end of *The Deer Park*, only O'Shaugnessy holds on to defiant art, while Faye holds out as the defiant spokesman on life.

O'Shaugnessy, the writer in training, has a thematic double in Faye, the man in training, and the latter's presence as a personal foil to the aesthetic problem in *The Deer Park* works in a theory at the roots of

Mailer's views on the artist—a theory which may explain why Mailer has taken on "the cult of personality." The theory assumes that the psychic gap between Norman Mailer the writer and Norman Mailer the man increased greatly following the super-success of *The Naked and the Dead,* a time when the lone alternative was to test a belief that "the first art work in an artist is the shaping of his own personality" (CC, 271).

At that time a condition similar to an alternating or dual personality sprung up within Mailer. There was no longer any correlation between the man whose character was being formed through experience and the writer whose talent was being developed through his art. The sudden fame had quickened and expanded Mailer's experiences as a man until personal growth began to outdistance artistic growth so much that Mailer lost the power to synthesize his life in his art: "I had the freak of luck to start high on the mountain and go down sharp while others were passing me. So I saw their faces as they learned to climb, and what faces they were! fear first with avidity up the ass; their steps—snobbery; the peak, power; and their terror-consequence" (ADV, 476–77). How to rid himself of any illusions concerning this sharp decline in artistic power became Mailer's most immediate problem.

His initial adjustment seems to have been to accept all possible experience as purely relative. If all directions tempt equally, only constant change makes for a strategy of success. "The first requirement of an interesting writer—one cannot predict his direction" (470). The "his" in this passage refers to Gore Vidal. Had Mailer been discussing only himself, he would have added, "one cannot predict his direction, *including himself*"—his way of conceding a temporary alienation between the writer and the man without discounting possibilities of mutual growth which would later unite them. Personal unpredictability can therefore lead either to success or failure. The latter takes place if the man becomes as unpredictable as the writer, interpreting his outer experience to be as chaotic as his own personality and talent. As a result the artist's persona would retrogress, becoming either a man living at the fullest intensity or a writer playing at dilettante nonsense. On the other hand, a successful outcome depends on whether the writer can become as predictable as the man once he declares his life journey to be chartless and uncertain. To give a preliminary stability and eventual predictability to the writer, the man must never fail to act on any possibility of drawing out aesthetic energy and personal meaning from an otherwise meaningless pattern of experience. He must realize that all incidents and situations change with the moment. Experience must be manipulated by the man who is unchanging and totally aware, sifting his every action and reaction to serve the needs of the writer within him. "Exceptional leverage" is Mailer's phrase to describe this tactic of the artist's persona: "Exceptional leverage upon the unconscious life in other people is the strength of the artist and the torment of the madman" (*PP*, 88). Mailer's continual exposure to "exceptional leverage" has taught him that the absolute control over one's thoughts and actions is the stuff of survival for a literary figure stuck in the limelight. As a result of years of self-made notoriety, Mailer's definition of "an interesting writer" also takes in a strategy of personality: "The first requirement of AN INTERESTING MAN—one cannot predict his direction *except himself*."

Mailer's style of ingrown honesty has also pushed self-awareness to a further awareness of "the real meaning of an artist" beyond the limits of any one-man "cult of personality." No artist can feel complete unless he takes action in public matters, a personal commitment that links artistic destiny with national destiny. What results is the artist as cultural spokesman—"artists embodied the essence of what was best in the nation, embodied it in their talent rather than in their character, which could be small, but their talent—this fruit of all that was rich and nourishing in their lives—was related directly to the dreams and the ambitions of the most imaginative part of the nation. So the destiny of a nation was not separate at all from the fate of its artists" (*PP*, 91). The artist as cultural spokesman can afford a "small" character so long as his talent keeps growing.

As a kind of afterpiece of the "cult of personality," *An American Dream* casts Mailer's talent and character in a new aesthetic mold. The Lovetts and O'Shaugnessys bogged down in aesthetic problems give way to a narrator who plays down the fact that he writes books on souped-up existentialism. Rojack instead resembles Marion Faye, a man whose brief time as a murderer leads to a technique in manners that transforms his life into art. Becoming a man (not a writer) spells out Rojack's pattern of survival. This novel, minus any trace of autobiography, seems rooted in Mailer's own "enormous present." As a result *An American Dream* becomes a novel of discovery as much for Mailer as for his readers. Much of Mailer's sense of discovery stems from a self-imposed ordeal at meeting eight serial deadlines for *Esquire*—a sure cure for recharging his energy after a nine year dry run with no novel. The serial form also seems to have made Mailer recheck Hemingway's message that "it was more important to be a man than a very good writer." Instead of Mailer living out a "cult of personality" pointed toward manhood, he begins to write it out; and in so doing, he discards the crutch of a fictional writer on a quest for manhood to make room for a new Mailer who fictionalizes what it is like to become a man. But in his switch to a more private world of the novel, Mailer does not turn autobiographical. Wild imagination rather than past experience shapes Rojack's dream, as Mailer internalizes events that could never happen to any one man. *An American Dream*—as a key to Mailer's more recent aesthetic views—has significance in terms of what Mailer no longer has to include or even mention. It reads as if Mailer has "muted" a further installment of *Advertisements* so much that even he can hardly hear it. When Roberts, dispensing with the usual police methods, tells Rojack—"I don't require that kind of leverage on you" (156)—Mailer seems to be echoing how he has revised his literary strategy by exerting more "exceptional leverage" on himself than on others. For this reason *An American Dream* marks the end of Mailer's leftover dream of being a man and then becoming a writer.

How Mailer will finally resolve his inner development as man and writer will come out in future novels or essays. An early (and still good) clue lies in his choosing to entitle the concluding section of his "muted autobiography," "Advertisements For Myself On The Way Out." This hints at the nature of his future work. Its "way out" themes should take on "the rude, the obscene, and the unsayable." But the term "out" also suggests the possibility of extending the self past the point of exhaustion and ultimately to oblivion or completion. Stretching before Mailer the man and Mailer the artist is this destination ambiguously labeled "out." What is being sought by Mailer in his literary future is maximum growth. For the writer this would result in increased talent and aesthetic energy, for the man, deeper meaning and personal fulfillment. This is the ideal—artist and man growing in total accord—but much depends on how well Mailer applies his egocentricity, courage and honesty toward his mission to create.

> it may be better to think of writers as pole vaulters than as artists . . . The writer, particularly the American writer, is not usually—if he is interesting—the quiet master of his craft; he is rather a being who ventured into the jungle of his unconscious to bring

back a sense of order or a sense of chaos; he passes through ambushes in his sleep, and if he is ambitious, he must be ready to engage the congealed hostility of the world. If a writer is really good enough and bold enough he will, by the logic of society, write himself out onto the end of a limb which the world will saw off. He does not go necessarily to his death, but he must dare it. (CC, 108)

Where does Mailer, this particular "pole-vaulter," land after writing himself" and living himself "out onto the end of a limb"? *An American Dream* shows that Mailer may be headed toward mysticism. In this connection, a passage from "A Calculus At Heaven," one of Mailer's earliest stories, ties the old to the new. He is describing the concluding times of Bowen Hilliard: "He had entered the army because at the end of his recapitulation of himself, he had come to the conclusion that to justify his life, to find some meaning in it would be possible only when he faced death . . . He had travelled the bridge from sensualism to mysticism, but he preferred it to cynicism" (ADV, 51). For the future Mailer, mysticism may be more necessary than preferable. Readapting his art to fit his life will make him realize now extreme his experience has become—an awareness that should result in writing which is more unworldly than worldly, more symbolic than literal, more private than public. Existentialism, scatology, cannibalism, incest, violence, magic, God and the Devil, pre-existence and the afterlife are some of the themes that should engage Mailer in the future. His role as cultural spokesman then will originate from an artistic vision based on personal contemplation. How good Mailer will be as a mystical writer "on the way in" will depend on how much "exceptional leverage" he can divert from "the unconscious life in other people" to the unconscious life within himself.

1

Early Last Words

My words on Mailer's future must pass for a whisper, after his first twenty years as the chameleon of American letters. I doubt whether Mailer (like a good existentialist) wants to see much beyond any enormous work-in-progress. Does this mean that Mailer will take to another twenty-year round of change, apparently for the sake of change? Apparently not, if old and recent signs are read. Mailer's persistent urge for a "big book" plus his deep-down "fondness for order" (CC, 220) suggest that constant change as literary strategy may soon reach its limits.

The clearest sign that Mailer's literary career will soon pass into a second and more crucial phase is his "new look." A more mellow and sweet Mailer emerges from Rojack's soft interludes with Cherry and Deirdre, and from such a warmed-over doubt as— "After all these years, I really don't know which is more important sexually, the orgasm or the family" (*Life*, Sept. 24, 1965). The family should win out. Beverly (Mailer's fourth and-I think-"ideal" wife) understands Norman and her part in a kind of marriage-as-mood. Besides, Beverly is the first to give Mailer a son, an image of self-perpetuation, and a graceful way to approach old age. Already the mood, like-father-like-son, is beginning—"But I've come to the middle-aged conclusion that I'm probably better as a writer than a man of action" (CC, 221). Chances are that Mailer's "cult of personality" will soon pass into an impersonal style of Papa Mailer. Once this happens, Mailer's art will keep time with its own "new look."

The key to Mailer's past work is a fear of repetition. Mailer has always aimed at a change in either subject or method or both. His tryouts include the novel, story, essay, journalism, interview, "muted autobiography," poetry and drama. All of Mailer's craze for literary experiment settles on one basic quest—for an authorial voice whose omniscience is tuned to the consciousness of his time.

In retrospect, Mailer's omniscience in *The Naked and the Dead* was a false start. His authorial voice echoed the pre-war rage for naturalism, a sound borrowed from Dos Passos, Dreiser, Hemingway. Readers and critics found it easy to identify with a familiar overview of a recent war, and Mailer's novel made it as an immediate best-seller blessed by the critics. But when Mailer saw the postwar scene grow enormous and complex, he could no longer find a voice big and deep enough to fit his vision, and he lost both sales and blessings when he put out *Barbary Shore*, with its near-allegory and vague narrator. Lovett—the "I" with a lost memory—was a stand-in spokesman for a writer with a lost voice.

Since then, Mailer has experimented with almost every aspect of his work, except with one kind of point of view. Omniscience remains his one taboo. He has not even explored third person limited omniscience (or what Henry James calls the "central intelligence") except in a few war stories (echoes of his first novel), and in "The Man Who Studied Yoga" where limited omniscience works well enough to make this Mailer's best fiction as fiction. But this quick slice of contemporary life falls short of any "big" vision. What is even worse in Mailer's view is the blend of irony and satire that makes up his stab at limited omniscience, a throwback to those "final sustaining ironies" of *The Naked and the Dead*. And so, "The Man Who Studied Yoga" becomes a false start of *The Deer Park* with still another "I" as storyteller. Even here Mailer comes as close to omniscience as he can. The "I" in the novel grows omniscient; and toward the end, the voice of O'Shaugnessy and Mailer almost merge. After *The Deer Park*, Mailer compensates for his failure to do omniscient fiction by turning to journalism and other nonfiction where an omniscient spokesman is judged by the facts of history, and not by the ideals of art. His much ado about that "big book" in *Advertisements* has more to do (than he wants to admit) with his greater need for a "big" voice.

In a roundabout way, Mailer admits this in his interview in *Paris Review* on "The Art of Fiction," reprinted in *Cannibals and Christians*. I say "roundabout" because Mailer is talking about how and what (not why) he writes. Unlike E. M. Forster who "had a developed view of the world," Mailer admits—"I would never be able to write in the third person until I developed a coherent view of life" (209). In the meantime, he is "doing a lot of different kinds of writing," or what he calls "keeping in shape" which is not the same as making it with craft—

> I think there's a natural mystique in the novel which is more important than craft. One is trying, after all, to capture reality, and that is extraordinarily and exceptionally difficult. I think craft is merely a series of way stations. . . . It is a grab bag of procedures, tricks, lore, formal gymnastics, symbolic superstructures, methodology in short. It's the compendium of what you've acquired from others. And since great writers communicate a vision of existence, one can't usually borrow their methods. The method is married to the vision. (*CC*, 215–16, 218)

In my view, Mailer's "method" and "vision" have split, but only temporarily, he hopes. An omniscient voice is his key to an ideal "method." To unite voice with vision, he has dropped an "adoration of craft" in favor of an absorption in change. Until he attains the "big book," all work-in-progress is expedient. Mailer may try to perfect such work by putting it "through the full gamut of (his) consciousness" (218), but I suspect that in a roundabout way his vision (minus a voice) takes the same trip.

One of Mailer's newer "waystations" for his vision is his use of the "treatment" in "The Last Night," "prophetic fiction" that closes *Cannibals and Christians*. As if "suggesting a motion picture to a (reader's) imagination" (381), a "treatment" does away with a developed story, depth characterization, and fresh and perceptive language. Instead, Mailer's "functional even cliché" language skims over the "pith and gist" of perhaps the most awesome subject —civilization's "last night" and possibly the "doom of the species" (268). Why does Mailer go out of his way to make the sublime sound banal? The answer is simple, in terms of how Mailer relates to the reader. A "treatment" makes Mailer's didactic tone almost glib, which should (as an afterthought) double a reader's sense of dread at such an offish view of his own end. Or a reader (familiar with Mailer's other work) may prefer to read this story as another ironic tribute to Hollywood for its many years of glossing over reality and debasing the language—its supporting role in the "last night." But Mailer's use of a "treatment" also plays a supporting role in how he relates to himself as writer. "The Last Night" is ideal stuff for a would-be Jeremiah. Here are the "roots" of many of Mailer's preoccupations—the destruction or salvation of civilization, the ultimate nature of power as either a pure expression for self or humanity, the limit-situation for existential politics, and so on. Here is that "big book" that never was. A "treatment" becomes a stand-in voice, a marriage of journalism and fiction, a makeshift omniscience, in the name of Mailer's search for a level of language to match the heights of his vision.

In his metaphysical "dialogues"—"The Metaphysics of the Belly" and "The Political Economy of Time"—Mailer's "new look" in method takes his search one step further. Again he has split his authorial voice in half, but in a more subtle way. As both interviewer and interviewee, Mailer has taken over the art of the interview. Along the lines of a divided omniscience between the author and his persona (or the "I") in his fiction, Mailer has created a dummy voice. His so-called dialogues are really Mailer talking to himself. But which one is the real Mailer? And, of course, the answer is either or neither—because his dual voice is a further extension of an "armature of (his) ego" for his most far-out trip into metaphysics. In these dialogues, there is much ado about the nature of aesthetics, scatology, cannibalism, food, form, time, death, soul, spirit, and all existence from the amoeba to the sardine to God. But Mailer warns his imaginary interviewer—"I don't begin to postulate. I offer you images, that is all" (*CC*, 332). And this is exactly what a reader receives—an associational stream of images, a purposive romp in metaphor with its "danger" that "contradictory meanings collect too easily about the core of meaning; unconnected meanings connect themselves" (308). This is part of Mailer's plan to make metaphors again "fit the vaults of modern experience" in the wake of science as a last ditch religion in which "experiment replaced the metaphor as a means of inquiry" (310, 308). Once a reader sees Mailer as a kind of "moral nihilist" of language, a larger question still remains: Is Mailer, as a metaphysician, being serious or playful? A choice depends on which tone a reader thinks he hears. Mailer protects himself well, by his tactics of split omniscience. He gives off unlimited possibilities of meaning by a blend of philosophical jargon and poetic imagery, a kind of verbal walk on a tightrope between sublimity and absurdity. If the former is heard, all has fallen well. If not, a reader will have to make room in the "art of the absurd" for a philosopher of the absurd. Besides, "metaphor exists to contain contradiction" (340) even between wisdom and tomfoolery. But Mailer's flair for a multiple tone still hints at a "contradiction" in himself, an authorial voice that cannot as yet be its own opposite. Just how much of Mailer's one-way dialogue—"The Political Economy of Time"—takes part in Rojack's one-way monologue depends on how well critics heed Mailer's "whisper"—"I would ask the reader to note how the interviewer and his subject get down to talking about the topics in *Cannibals and Christians* and—I whisper it—*An American Dream.* (*CC*, 261). Until Mailer's omniscient voice turns into more than a whisper, readers and critics may prefer to think Mailer's vision is too "big" for any one voice. In that case, Mailer's failure of language rests on him as much as on his times.

After his rapport with naturalism and his omniscient voice gave out, Mailer cocked his eye on the American scene and saw "that the romantic spirit (had) dried up, that there (was) almost no shame today, like the terror before the romantic" (*ADV*, 382). His new mission was to expose this shame; and his image took to the dark side of romanticism. He became a kind of Coleridge or Byron in the raw and on the loose during the computer age—a modern Hawthorne faced with a time when all letters run from A to Z in toneless grays.

Mailer's vision during these years crystallized into one belief—that America has never had its own soul. History (one of Mailer's "big" words) explained why America's roots were entirely material. This was not the case with Europe. When the Industrial Revolution hit Europe, it had a spiritual heritage to blend with the new craze for materialism. But America was old before it was young, as European culture came over, in the guise of a New World. A frontier Adam might have owned a borrowed soul, but he still moved better with his body, and the Industrial Revolution became America's short cut for making a wilderness into a metropolis. Without any spiritual backlog of its own, a young America took over materialism and perfected it into a stand-in religion. The frontier closed on a soulless nation, crammed with things made over into a Dream. After World War II (Mailer's time), America emerged as a mod version of Rome, with its Athens and Calvary a vague part of a European satellite, foreign and out of sight. History had seldom recorded such awkwardness, as America dumped its style of power morality (a mixed bag of computers, missiles and Christianity) on the world scene. Mailer saw how America's consciousness kept using money and other things to avoid the unpleasantness of super weapons half used and spiritual truths half believed. Mailer's America became a land where cannibals and Christians passed for each other, where the materials of self-destruction had outgrown any moral capacity for survival. No matter how universal Mailer's voice sounded—"But the war between being and nothingness is the underlying illness of the twentieth century" (CC, 214)—the fact remained that for twenty years Mailer's work had been a "peculiarly American statement." When he hinted at his present and future "obsession with how God exists" (CC, 214), he was whispering a historical fact—a "plague" or "cancer" or "totalitarianism" or "barbarism" or whatever guise it takes—that America has had everything but a soul.

During his first twenty years of literary life, Mailer has evolved into an American Jeremiah in search of a voice that would justify his role. At present, the language of existentialism enables Mailer to keep his voice in tune with the times. But he realizes that this language is a borrowed omniscience, echoes of Sartre, Heidegger, Jaspers and others. Mailer may "admire" Sartre and Heidegger for "their formidable powers," but he still "suspect(s) they are no closer to the buried continent of existentialism than were medieval cartographers near to a useful map of the world. The new continent which shows on our psychic maps as intimations of eternity is still to be discovered" (CC, 215). In this Wordsworthian whisper to a computer age, there is a hint that Mailer's rapport with the language of existentialism will soon end. An unbor-rowed language may be the only way to "discover" a "new continent." In the meantime, Mailer's word on "our psychic maps" must wait for a voice that re-sounds rather than whispers.

Mailer's next twenty years of literary life should move at a speedy clip. As long as he fails to unite vision and language, there will be more "I" narrators, mock-dialogues and other forms of a split-voice done up in a rugged romanticism. A chameleon (by choice) must stay prolific, until his method catches up with his subject. In the good old past, Mailer's quest would fall in with the grail—the Great American Novel. Maybe, a "big book" is Mailer's early word on yester-day's ideal in American letters, an updated and over-sized dream of a synthesis of all genres—drama, po-etry, fiction, essays, even journalism. Here, then, would be the gist of Mailer's "keeping in shape," running all genres "through the gamut of (his) con-sciousness," so that he can do them all at once. Such a book (if this is Mailer's ideal) already may be too "big" for any one writer. An early word can end up far from last. I wonder if that "big book" has or will lose all value for Mailer the writer, and instead evolve into a dramatic device by which Mailer the man keeps in top shape through the ultimate challenge of doing the impossible. For if his "big book" were ever written, after all the critics swooned over a new and improved *The Naked and the Dead* and after all his disciples and detractors yelled "me too," what would be left for Mailer but a literary career at an end too soon.

Selected Bibliography

Works by Mailer: BOOKS

Advertisements For Myself. New York: G. P. Putnam's Sons, 1959.
An American Dream. New York: The Dial Press, 1965.
Barbary Shore. New York: Rinehart and Co., 1951.
Cannibals and Christians. New York: The Dial Press, 1966.
Deaths for the Ladies and Other Disasters. New York: G. P. Putnam's Sons, 1962.
The Deer Park. New York: G. P. Putnam's Sons, 1955.
The Naked and the Dead. New York: Rinehart and Co., 1948.
The Presidential Papers. New York: G. P. Putnam's Sons, 1963.

Biographical and Critical Sources

Aldridge, John W. *After the Lost Generation.* New York: McGraw-Hill Book Co., 1951.
————. *In Search of Heresy.* New York: McGraw-Hill Book Co., 1956.
————. *Time to Murder and Create.* New York: David McKay Co., Inc., 1966.
————. "What Became of Our Postwar Hopes?" *New York Times Book Review* (July 29, 1962), 1, 24. Reprinted as "The War Writers Ten Years Later" in *Contemporary American Novelists.* Edited by Harry T. Moore. Carbondale: Southern Illinois University Press, 1964.
Alvarez, A. "Norman X," *Spectator,* No. 7141 (May 7, 1965), 603.
"Americana: Of Time & The Rebel," *Time,* LXXVI (December 5, 1960), 16–17.

Auchincloss, Eve and Nancy Lynch. "An Interview with Norman Mailer," *Mademoiselle*, LII (February 1961), 76–77, 160–63.

"Authors: Two Bucks—20 Dances," *Newsweek*, LIX (March 12, 1962), 104.

"Backstage with Esquire," *Esquire*, LIV (November 1960), 75–76.

"Backstage with Esky," *Esquire*, XXXIX (April 1953), 15–16.

Balakian, Nona. "The Prophetic Vogue of the Anti-heroine," *Southwest Review*, XLVII (Spring 1962), 134–41.

Baldwin, James. "The Black Boy Looks at the White Boy," *Esquire*, LV (May 1961), 102–6. Reprinted in *Nobody Knows My Name*. New York: The Dial Press, 1961.

Beaver, Harold. "A Figure in the Carpet: Irony and the American Novel," *Essays and Studies*, XV (1962), 101–14.

"The Boston Trial of *Naked Lunch*," *Evergreen Review* (June 1965), 40–49; 87–88.

Breit, Harvey. "Talk with Norman Mailer," *The New York Times Book Review*, LVI (June 3, 1951), 20. Reprinted in *The Writer Observed*. Cleveland and New York: The World Publishing Co., 1956, 199–201.

Breslow, Paul. "The Hipster and the Radical," *Studies on the Left*, I:3 (1960), 102–5.

Brower, Brock. "*In This Corner*, Norman Mailer, Never the Champion, Always the Challenger," *Life*, 59:13 (September 24, 1965), 94–117.

Brustein, Robert. "Who's Killing the Novel?" *New Republic*, CLII (October 23, 1965), 22–24.

Bryant, Jerry H. "The Last of the Social Protest Writers," *Arizona Quarterly*, XIX (Winter, 1963), 315–25.

Christian, Frederick. "The Talent and the Torment," *Cosmopolitan*, CLV (August 1963), 63–67.

Cleaver, Eldridge. "Notes on a Native Son," *Ramparts*, V (June 1966), 51–56.

Cook, Bruce A. "Norman Mailer: The Temptation to Power," *Renascence*, XIV (Summer 1962), 206–15, 222.

Corrington, John William. "An American Dreamer," *Chicago Review*, 18:1, (1965), 58–66.

Cowley, Malcolm. "The Literary Situation 1965 (A Seminar at the Southern Literary Festival)," *University of Mississippi Studies in English*, VI (1965), 91–98.

Culey, Thomas F. "The Quarrel with Time in American Fiction," *American Scholar*, XXIX (Autumn 1960), 552, 554, 556, 558, 560.

Current Biography: 1948. New York: H. W. Wilson Co., 1948, 408–10.

De Mott, Benjamin. "Docket No. 15883," *American Scholar*, XXX (Spring 1961), 232–37.

Didion, Joan. "A Social Eye," *National Review*, XVII (April 20, 1965), 329–30.

Dienstfrey, Harris. "Norman Mailer." *On Contemporary Literature*. Edited by Richard Kostelanetz. New York: Avon Books (1964), 422–36.

Donohue, H. E. F. *Conversations with Nelson Algren*. New York: Hill and Wang, 1964.

Downes, Robin Nelson. *A Bibliography of Norman Mailer*. Tallahassee, Florida State University, 1957 (Available only on microcard).

Duhamel, P. Albert. "Love in the Modern Novel," *Catholic World*, 191:1141 (April 1960), 31–35.

Dupee, F. W. "The American Norman Mailer," *Commentary*, XXIX (February 1960), 128–32.

Elsinger, Chester E. *Fiction of the Forties*. Chicago & London: The University of Chicago Press, 1963.

Fiedler, Leslie A. "The Breakthrough: The American Jewish Novelist and the Fictional Image of the Jew," *Midstream*, IV (Winter 1958), 15–35. Reprinted in *Recent American Fiction*. Edited by Joseph J. Waldmeir. Boston: Houghton Mifflin Company, 1963, 84–109.

———. "Caliban or Hamlet: An American Paradox," *Encounter*, XXVI (April 1966), 23–27.

———. *Waiting For The End*. New York: Stein and Day, 1964.

Finkelstein, Sidney. *Existentialism and Alienation in American Literature*. New York: International Publishers, Co., 1965.

———. "Norman Mailer and Edward Albee," *American Dialog*, II (February-March 1965), 23–28.

Fuller, Edmund. *Man in Modern Fiction*. New York: Random House, 1958.

Geismar, Maxwell. *American Moderns: From Rebellion to Conformity.* New York: Hill and Wang, 1958.

Gelfant, Blanche H. *The American City Novel.* Norman, Oklahoma: University of Oklahoma Press, 1954.

Gilman, Richard. "Why Mailer Wants To Be President," *New Republic,* CL (February 8, 1964), 17–20; 22–24.

Girson, Rochella. "'48's Nine," *Saturday Review of Literature,* XXXII (February 12, 1949), 12–14.

Glicksberg, Charles I. "Norman Mailer: The Angry Young Novelist in America," *Wisconsin Studies in Contemporary Literature,* I (Winter 1960), 25–34.

———. "Sex in Contemporary Literature," *Colorado Quarterly,* IX (Winter 1961), 277–87.

Gold, Herbert. "How To Tell the Beatniks From the Hipsters," *The Noble Savage,* No. 1 (Spring 1960), 132–39.

Goldman, Lawrence. "The Political Vision of Norman Mailer," *Studies on the Left,* IV (Summer 1964), 129–41.

Goldstone, Herbert. "The Novels of Norman Mailer," *The English Journal,* XLV (March 1956), 113–21.

Guttmann, Allen. "Jewish Radicals, Jewish Writers," *American Scholar,* XXXII (Autumn 1963), 563–75.

Hampshire, Stuart. "Mailer United," *New Statesman and Nation* (October 13, 1961), 515–16.

Hassen, Ihab. *Radical Innocence: Studies in the Contemporary American Novel.* Princeton, N. J.: Princeton University Press, 1961.

———. "The Way Down and Out," *Virginia Quarterly Review,* XXXIX (Winter 1963), 81–93.

Hastings, Michael. "Who Is Killing Us?" *Time and Tide,* XLII (October 12, 1961), 1704.

Healy, Robert C. "Novelists of the War: A Bunch of Dispossessed." *Fifty Years of the American Novel: A Christian Appraisal.* Edited by Harold C. Gardiner, S.J. New York: Charles Scribner's Sons, 1952.

Hoffman, Frederick J. *The Immortal No: Death and the Modern Imagination.* Princeton, New Jersey: Princeton University Press, 1964.

———. *The Modern Novel in America.* Chicago: Henry Regnery Co., 1963.

————. "Norman Mailer and the Revolt of the Ego: Some Observations on Recent American Literature," *Wisconsin Studies in Contemporary Literature,* I (Autumn 1961), 5–12.

Howe, Irving. "Mass Society and Post-Modern Fiction," *Partisan Review,* XXVI (Summer 1959), 420–36.

————. "A Quest for Peril: Norman Mailer." *A World More Attractive*: *A View of Modern Literature and Politics.* New York: Horizon Press, 1963, 123–29.

Hyman, Stanley E. *Standards*: *A Chronicle of Books for our Time.* New York: Horizon Press, 1966.

Jones, James. "Small Comment from a Penitent Novelist," *Esquire,* LX (December 1963), 40, 44.

Kazin, Alfred. "How Good Is Norman Mailer?" *The Reporter,* XXI (November 26, 1959), 40–41. Reprinted in *Contemporaries.* Boston: Little, Brown, 1962, 246–50.

————. "Imagination and the Age," *The Reporter,* 34:9 (May 5, 1966), 32–35.

————. "The Jew as Modern Writer," *Commentary,* 41:4 (April 1966), 37–41.

Kermode, Frank. "Rammel," *New Statesman,* LXIX:1783 (May 14, 1965), 765–66.

Krim, Seymour. "A Hungry Mental Lion," *Evergreen Review,* IV (January-February 1960), 178–85.

Lakin, R. D. "The Displaced Writer in America," *Midwest Quarterly,* IV (Summer 1963), 295–303.

Land, Myrick Ebben. *The Fine Art of Literary Mayhem.* New York: Holt, 1963.

Lasch, Christopher. *The New Radicalism in America, 1889–1963*: *The Intellectual as a Social Type.* New York: Knopf, 1965.

Lebowitz, Naomi. *The Imagination of Loving.* Detroit: Wayne State University Press, 1965.

Leffelaar, H. L. "Norman Mailer in Chicago," *Litterair Paspoort,* XV (April 1960), 79–81.

Lewis, R. W. B. "Recent Fiction: Picaro and Pilgrim." *A Time of Harvest*: *American Literature 1910–1960.* Edited by Robert E. Spiller. New York: Hill and Wang, 1962, 144–53.

Ludwig, Jack. *Recent American Novelists.* Minneapolis: University of Minnesota Press, 1962.

MacDonald, Dwight. "Art, Life and Violence," *Commentary*, XXXIII (June 1962), 169–72.

––––––. "The Bright Young Men in the Arts," *Esquire*, L (September 1958), 38–40.

––––––. "Our Far-Flung Correspondents: Massachusetts vs. Mailer," *The New Yorker*, XXXVI (October 8, 1960), 154–66.

Malin, Irving and Irwin Stark, editors. *Breakthrough*: A *Treasury of Contemporary American-Jewish Literature*. New York: McGraw-Hill, 1964.

Malin, Irving. *Jews and Americans*. Carbondale: Southern Illinois University Press, 1965.

Millgate, Michael. *American Social Fiction*. New York: Barnes & Noble, 1964.

Mudrick, Marvin. "Mailer and Styron: Guests of the Establishment," *The Hudson Review*, XVII (Autumn 1964), 346–66.

Nedelin, V. " 'War Lovers' and Their Victims," *Ionstrannaja Literatura*, No. 7 (July 1961), 171–84.

Newfield, Jack. "Bobby Hero," *Cavalier*, 16:4 (August 1966), 31, 82–85.

Nyren, Dorothy, editor. A *Library of Literary Criticism*. *Modern American Literature*. New York: Frederick Ungar Publishing Co., 1964, 312–15.

PPA Press Conference: Summary for *Publisher's Weekly*, 187 (March 22, 1965), 42, 44–45.

Podhoretz, Norman. "Norman Mailer: The Embattled Vision," *Partisan Review*, XXVI (Summer 1959), 371–91. Reprinted as "Introduction" to *Barbary Shore*. New York: The Universal Library: Grosset & Dunlap, 1963. Reprinted in *Recent American Fiction*: *Some Critical Views*. Edited by Joseph J. Waldmeir. Boston: Houghton Mifflin Company, 1963. Reprinted in *Doings and Undoings*: *The Fifties and After in American Writing*. New York: Farrar, Strauss, 1964.

Prescott, Orville. *In My Opinion*. Indianapolis, Ind.: Bobbs-Merrill Co., 1952.

Rahv, Philip. *The Myth and the Powerhouse*. New York: Farrar, Strauss and Giroux, 1965.

Richler, Mordecai. "Norman Mailer," *Encounter*, XXV (July 1965), 61–64.

Rideout, Walter B. *The Radical Novel in the United*

States 1900–1954. Cambridge, Mass.: Harvard University Press, 1956.

"Rugged Times," *New Yorker*, XXIV (October 23, 1948), 25.

Samuels, Charles T. "Mailer vs. the Hilton Hotel," *National Review*, XVIII (October 18, 1966), 1059–62.

Schrader, George Alfred. "Norman Mailer and the Despair of Defiance," *The Yale Review*, LI (Winter 1962), 267–80.

Scott, James Burton. *The Individual and Society: Norman Mailer versus William Styron*. Syracuse: Syracuse University, 1964 (Available on microfilm and xerography).

Shaw, Peter. "The Tough Guy Intellectual," *Critical Quarterly*, VIII (Spring 1966), 13–28.

Siegel, Jules. "Norman Mailer vs. Dickens, Dostoevsky and Others," *Cavalier*, 15:7 (January 1966), 57–58, 90.

Skellings, Edmund, editor. "Mailer in Provincetown," *Author-Interview Tape Library*.

———. "Mailer in Alaska," *Author-Interview Tape Library*.

Spender, Stephen. "Mailer's American Melodrama." *The Great Ideas Today, 1965*. Edited by Robert M. Hutchins and Mortimer J. Adler. Chicago: Encyclopaedia Britannica, Inc., 1965.

Steiner, George. "Naked But Not Dead," *Encounter*, XVII (December 1961), 67–70.

Stevenson, David L. "Styron and the Fiction of the Fifties," *Critique*, III (Summer 1960), 47–58.

Swados, Harvey. "Must Writers Be Characters?" *Saturday Review*, XLIII (October 1, 1960), 12–14, 50.

Tanner, Tony. "The Great American Nightmare," *Spectator*, No. 7192 (April 29, 1966), 530–31.

Thorp, Willard. *American Writing in the Twentieth Century*. Cambridge: Harvard University Press, 1963.

Trilling, Diana. "Norman Mailer," *Encounter*, XIX (November 1962), 45–56. Reprinted as "The Radical Moralism of Norman Mailer" in *The Creative Present*. Edited by Nona Balakian and Charles Simmons. New York: Doubleday and Co., 1963. Reprinted in *Claremont Essays*. New York: Harcourt, Brace & World, 1964, 175–202.

Twentieth Century Authors, First Supplement. Edited by Stanley J. Kunitz. New York: H. W. Wilson Co., 1955, 628–29.

Vidal, Gore. "The Norman Mailer Syndrome," *The Nation*, CXC (January 2, 1960), 13–16.

Vlaamse, Gids. "Niuw Vooruitstrevend Amerikaans Proza," *Visvabharati Quarterly*, XLV (November 1961), 751–56.

Volpe, Edmond L. "James Jones—Norman Mailer." *Contemporary American Novelists*. Edited by Harry T. Moore. Carbondale, Ill.: Southern Illinois University Press, 1964, 106–19.

Waldmeir, Joseph J. "Accommodations in the New Novel," *University College Quarterly*, XI (November 1965), 26–32.

Warfel, Harry R. *American Novelists of Today*. New York: American Book Co., 1951.

Weber, Brom. "A Fear of Dying: Norman Mailer's *An American Dream*," *Hollins Critic*, II (June 1965), 1–6, 8–11.

Widmer, Kingsley. "The Hollywood Image," *Coastlines*, V (Autumn 1961), 17–27.

———. *The Literary Rebel*. Carbondale and Edwardsville: Southern Illinois University Press, 1965.

Willingham, Calder. "The Way It Isn't Done: Notes on the Distress of Norman Mailer," *Esquire*, LX (December 1963), 306–8.

Wilson, Robert Anton. "Negative Thinking: The New Art of the Brave," *Realist*, No. 22 (December 1960), 5, 11–13.

Winegarten, Renee. "Norman Mailer—Genuine or Counterfeit?" *Midstream*, XI (September 1965), 91–95.

Wood, Margery. "Norman Mailer and Nathalie Sarraute: A Comparison of Existential Novels," *Minnesota Review*, VI:1 (1966), 67–72.

Woodress, James. "The Anatomy of Recent Fiction Reviewing, *Midwest Quarterly*, II (Autumn 1960), 67–81.

Index